step-by-step cooking

CHINESE

delightful ideas for everyday meals

step-by-step cooking

CHINESE

delightful ideas for everyday meals

 Marshall Cavendish
Cuisine

The Publisher wishes to thank Robinson & Co., (Singapore) Pte Ltd for the loan of their crockery and utensils.

Photographer: Sam Yeo
Food Preparation: Sharon Soh

First published 2005 as Feast of Flavours from the Chinese Kitchen
This new edition 2011

© 2005 Marshall Cavendish International (Asia) Private Limited

Published by Marshall Cavendish Cuisine
An imprint of Marshall Cavendish International

Other Marshall Cavendish Offices:
Marshall Cavendish International. PO Box 65829 London EC1P 1NY, UK ▪ Marshall Cavendish Corporation. 99 White Plains Road, Tarrytown NY 10591-9001, USA ▪ Marshall Cavendish International (Thailand) Co Ltd. 253 Asoke, 12th Flr, Sukhumvit 21 Road, Klongtoey Nua, Wattana, Bangkok 10110, Thailand ▪ Marshall Cavendish (Malaysia) Sdn Bhd, Times Subang, Lot 46, Subang Hi-Tech Industrial Park, Batu Tiga, 40000 Shah Alam, Selangor Darul Ehsan, Malaysia

Marshall Cavendish is a trademark of Times Publishing Limited

National Library Board Singapore Cataloguing in Publication Data

Chinese : delightful ideas for everyday meals. – New ed. – Singapore :
Marshall Cavendish Cuisine, 2011.
p. cm. – (Step-by-step cooking series)
Includes index.
ISBN : 978-981-4328-76-0

1. Cooking, Chinese. I. Series: Step-by-step cooking series (Marshall Cavendish Cuisine)

TX724.5.C5
641.5951 -- dc22   OCN683402344

Printed in Singapore by KWF Printing Pte Ltd.

CONTENTS

INTRODUCTION

Cooking Techniques   6
Cooking Utensils   10
Weights & Measures   13

STARTERS

Fried Meat and Vegetable Dumplings   16
Deep-fried Pork Rolls   18
Steamed Mushrooms with Prawn Filling   20
Stuffed Capsicums (Bell Peppers)   22
Deep-fried Five-spice Rolls   24

SOUPS

Duck and Salted Vegetable Soup   28
Old Cucumber and Pork Soup   30
Bean Curd Hot Pot   32
Hot Sour Soup   34
Prawn Wantan Soup   36

SEAFOOD

Stir-Fried Sichuan Style Squid   40
Chilli Oyster Crabs   42
Sea Bass with Spicy Black Vinegar Sauce   44
Butter Prawns with Toasted Coconut   46
Crab Omelette   48
Fried Oyster Fritters   50
Braised Fish with Black Bean Sauce   52
Claypot Fish Head   54

MEAT & POULTRY

Beef Patties in Tomato Sauce   58
Chicken Stew with Fresh Chestnuts   60
Fried Garlic Pork   62
Five-spice Crispy Skin Chicken   64
Pig's Trotters in Chinese Black Vinegar   66
Ginger Chicken in Earthen Pot   68
Teochew Duck   70
Roast Pork Ribs   72

VEGETABLES

Stir-fried Prawns with Cloud Ear
   Fungus and Snow Peas   76
Stir-fried Sweet and Sour Cabbage   78
Braised Dried Bean Curd with
   Dried Chinese Mushrooms   80
Bean Sprouts and Carrot with Salted Fish   82
Stir-fried Aubergines (Eggplants)
   with Minced Meat   84

RICE & NOODLES

Fried Yellow Noodles with Meat
   and Prawns   88
Fried Flat Rice Noodles with Beef   90
Rice Porridge   92
Fried Rice   94
Transparent Noodles and Fish Ball Soup   96
Steamed Chicken Glutinous Rice (Lor Ma Kai)   98
Pork Chow Mien   100

SWEETS

Gingko Nut and Water Chestnut Dessert   104
Sweet Dumplings   106
Sweet Yam Paste (Au Nee)   108
Peanut Crème   110

GLOSSARY & INDEX

Glossary   112
Index   119

COOKING TECHNIQUES

Chinese cuisine has developed numerous cooking methods to make the most out of the variety of foods and ingredients available in the vast country. Ingredients and methods vary from region to region and often, there will be regional differences in the preparation of the same dishes.

Basic techniques of Chinese cooking include precooking techniques such as parboiling and partial frying and cooking techniques such as frying, sautéing, braising, stewing, boiling, simmering, steaming, 'flavour-potting' and smoking.

PRECOOKING METHODS

Precooking meats gets rid of off-odours while precooking vegetables gets rid of astringency or bitterness and highlights their fresh colour. Usually, ingredients are either parboiled or partially fried first before they are combined with other ingredients.

BOILING

There are four methods of boiling, namely parboiling, slow-boiling, hot-plunging or blanching, and quick-boiling. Each method produces a different result.

PARBOILING

Vegetables such as taro root, Chinese yams and fresh bamboo shoots have to be parboiled by cooking in boiling water to remove their astringent taste. Parboiling also makes peeling much easier.

SLOW-BOILING

Slow-boiling is used to prepare ingredients that have a longer cooking time than other ingredients in the same recipe, such as pork tripe. To slow-boil, simmer the ingredient in boiling water until tender then add to the rest of the ingredients.

HOT-PLUNGING OR BLANCHING

Hot-plunging or blanching is used to retain the colour and texture of tender and fresh vegetables, such as celery, spinach and green beans. First plunge vegetables

INTRODUCTION

into a pot of boiling water and remove when the water starts to boil again. Drain and run under cold water immediately.

QUICK-BOILING

Quick-boiling can get rid of the blood odour and small bits of bone from the meat. To quick-boil meat, place the meat in cold water and bring to the boil. Remove and drain once the water starts to boil. To quick-boil pig kidney, fish and chicken, plunge into boiling water and remove once it is cooked.

PARTIAL FRYING

There are two methods of partial frying in Chinese cooking.

SLIDING THROUGH THE OIL

Sliding through the oil means placing an ingredient in warm oil at 70–100°C (160–210°F) for just long enough to seal in the juices.

GOING THROUGH THE OIL

Going through the oil means deep-frying an ingredient, usually a meat, in hot oil at 110–170°C (230–340°F) until partially or thoroughly cooked, depending on what is desired.

COOKING TEMPERATURES

Temperature control is an essential technique in Chinese cooking because different temperatures and cooking times produce different results.

In Chinese recipes, there are three kinds of heat: high heat, used in stir-frying, quick-frying and deep-frying; medium heat, used in sautéing, slippery-frying and deep-frying coated food; and low heat, used in steaming, simmering, braising and stewing.

High heat is used for producing a fast boil, where the water or liquid is kept bubbling, for hot-plunging and quick-boiling. It is also used for reducing broths and stocks.

Medium heat is used for keeping liquids at a moderate boil in some types of braising.

Low heat is used for keeping liquids at a slow boil or at a simmer during stewing, simmering and 'flavour-potting'.

COOKING WITH OIL

Oil is warm when no bubbles appear around a small piece of vegetable leaf or a slice of ginger that has been tossed into the oil.

Oil is moderately hot when small bubbles sizzle around a piece of ginger that has been tossed into the oil.

Oil is very hot when a 3-cm (1-in) cube of day-old bread turns brown in 1 minute when dropped into the oil.

Oil is boiling hot when a heavy haze appears and the oil bubbles vigorously.

Most recipes require either hot or very hot oil. Oil at lower temperatures are used for partial frying while extremely hot oil is used for crisping and browning coated foods that have already been fried at a lower temperature.

COATING

There are a few types of coating used in Chinese cooking. The most common one is made of two parts corn flour and one part water. It is usually used in slippery-frying and deep-frying.

Other popular coatings include an egg and breadcrumb coating and a flour and egg yolk coating. These 2 coatings require two-step preparation. For the former, dip into beaten egg yolk then roll in breadcrumbs. For the latter, dip into flour then into beaten egg yolk.

STIR-FRYING

Stir-frying is one of the most famous methods of Chinese cooking but it is also the most difficult because speed and control is critical in ensuring success.

In stir-frying, food is cooked quickly at high temperatures in order to preserve its natural colour and texture, especially vegetables. Stir-frying meat seals in the juices prior to further cooking. It is a healthy method of cooking since very little oil is used.

When stir-frying, make sure that you use a good source of heat that can be easily adjusted. The gas cooker is recommended for its ease of control and practicality. On the other hand, electric hot plates are unsuitable for stir-frying because of poor heat control.

IMPORTANT NOTES TO REMEMBER:

1. Prepare all ingredients before starting to stir-fry.
2. Cut ingredients into similar sized small cubes or slices so that they cook quickly and evenly.
3. Heat the wok before adding oil and make sure that the oil is really hot before you add the ingredients.

4. To flavour the oil, fry garlic and shallots until fragrant and lightly browned before adding the remaining ingredients.
5. Stir ingredients constantly to ensure even cooking.
6. Be careful not to overcook.
7. Use simple garnishes.

BOILING (POH, SAP AND LUK)

Boiling may seem to be the simplest cooking method but in Chinese cooking, there are as many as three different degrees of boiling, namely *poh*, *sap* and *luk*. The most commonly used one is *poh*, where a plentiful amount of stock or water is rapidly boiled for a brief period. The heat is then reduced to allow it to simmer for a couple of hours. A considerable amount of stock or water is left behind, unlike in braising and stewing. *Poh* is used for making porridge, rice and soups but when cooking rice, you have to cook until all the liquid is absorbed by the rice.

Sap is done by placing meat into rapidly boiling water briefly. Sometimes, the meat is allowed to cook further by leaving it in the hot water with the heat turned off. The cooked meat can be served marinated, covered with a sauce or with a dip. Getting the right timing is critical to the success of this method, and anybody who has tried preparing Hainanese chicken rice will definitely attest to that.

The third variation is *luk*, which is mainly used for cooking green leafy vegetables and noodles by scalding quickly in boiling water or stock. All sorts of green leafy vegetables can be cooked this way then mixed with oil and sauces, preserving their natural crunchiness. Noodles can also be prepared with this method, then either mixed with sauce and served with meat on top or served in soup. *Luk* softens egg noodles and gets rid of excess starch prior to stir-frying.

Meat, cut into small pieces or shredded to ensure adequate scalding, can also be prepared in this way. When scalded properly, the flavour and marinade will be sealed inside. This method is useful for preparing meat for soups so that scum will not form.

IMPORTANT NOTES TO REMEMBER:

1. Use a wok or pot that can contain enough water to immerse the food. The water must be boiling before the food is added.
2. Watch the duration of cooking time and adjust heat accordingly to avoid overcooking.
3. When boiling for a long duration, make sure that there is adequate water or stock in the pot. Top up accordingly if needed.

4. To prevent vegetables or noodles from overcooking, use a wire mesh ladle to scoop them out of the pot quickly.
5. After vegetables and noodles are done, quickly plunge into cold water to stop cooking then drain well. This helps to retain the fresh green colour of the vegetables.
6. Garnish boiled dishes simply with some chopped spring onions, coriander leaves and chillies.

SHALLOW-FRYING

When shallow-frying, the food is cooked with a small amount of oil and the food is hardly moved around so as to produce a crispy outer layer while keeping the inside moist. The natural flavour is also retained. This method is used for cooking fish, eggs, dumplings, stuffed vegetables and any foods that cook easily. Food prepared this way is usually served with a variety of dips and garnished with colourful vegetables and fruits to make the plain fried dish more attractive.

Use a flat pan for shallow-frying so that the oil can be evenly spread out and heated up before adding the food. This prevents food from sticking. Control the temperature and watch the timing carefully to prevent overcooking. Start by cooking on high heat for a few seconds, then turn down to medium or low heat, depending on the thickness of the food.

DEEP-FRYING

To deep-fry food, the food has to be immersed in very hot oil. This produces a very crispy outside, especially when cooking poultry and seafood. Deep-fried food can either be marinated or coated with a batter, then served with a dip or covered with a cooked sauce.

To prevent overcooking, carefully regulate the temperature and observe the timing of the cooking period. Use a wok for deep-frying so that the food can be totally immersed in oil or partly immersed with enough room for basting.

STEAMING

To steam food, place the food above boiling water and let the heat from the steam cook the food. It is an easy, fast and clean method of cooking. Although the method is simple, the correct marinade has to be carefully chosen to produce the desired flavour and texture.

Steaming is good for meat, fish and prawn dishes. When done, add garnishing to bring out the flavour and make the dish more attractive. You can use garnishing such as red chilli flowers, spring onions soaked in cold water for curling effect or a bunch of coriander leaves to make the dish more colourful.

IMPORTANT NOTES TO REMEMBER:

1. Use a metal steamer with a tight-fitting lid. Make sure the steamer is big enough for the food. The amount of water required depends on the length of steaming period but as a general guide, fill the steamer up to the halfway mark of the bottom pan. Top up with boiling water accordingly when there is not enough water to finish the steaming.
2. Make sure that the water in the steamer is at a rapid boil before putting in the food.
3. Whenever the cover is opened, wipe the underside dry to prevent condensed water from dripping onto the food. Alternatively, a dry towel can be placed under the lid to prevent dripping.
4. All meat and seafood should be marinated before steaming, for at least 15 minutes. When using a thickening, always stir the food again just before steaming to prevent lumps from forming.
5. When steamed for the correct length of time, the resulting texture will be very smooth. Oversteamed egg dishes will produce watery, coarse and pockmarked texture.
   There is another method of steaming called 'double steaming' or 'closed steaming'. The difference is that the steaming is done in a closed stoneware pot. Sometimes, the Chinese will scoop out the insides of whole coconuts, winter melons and pumpkins so that they can be used as pots to prepare herbal soups with added flavour. This method is mainly used for preparing herbal soups, usually with expensive herbs and ingredients.

BRAISING AND STEWING

This is a long cooking process which takes up to several hours. Meat, seafood and vegetables are slowly simmered together with a variety of sauces and spices to create delicious Chinese dishes with rich sauces and wonderful aromas.

The success of braising and stewing depends on the combination of sauces, ingredients and spices used. Light and dark soy sauces are essential ingredients. Ginger, garlic and shallots give flavour while popular spices used include five-spice powder, cinnamon, clove, star anise and Sichuan and white peppercorns. It is a good idea to wrap all the spices in a muslin bag so that the spices can be easily removed as required and prevent the spices from clouding the sauce.

Before braising, make sure the meat has been marinated for some time so that it can absorb all the seasoning. You can also seal in flavour and juices of meat and vegetables by frying quickly in oil or by blanching in boiling water.

Keep the garnishing very simple for braised dishes, some chopped spring onion or topping of coriander or parsley will suffice.

Usually, the earthen pot or clay pot is used because of they are better for slow cooking. The wok is also used, especially for whole fowls, fish and large cuts of meat. When braising, applying too much heat will ruin the dish. It is easier to use an electric crockpot for braising and stewing.

ROASTING AND GRILLING

Traditionally, roasting in Chinese cooking is done either on an open or closed spit. Nowadays, the conventional oven is used. Chinese roasted pig, duck and goose with crispy skin and tasty meat are famous all over the world. For the best roasted meats, you have to use a closed, turning drum-shaped spit that is fired by charcoal. A variation is dry-roasting in a wok filled with coarse salt. This method is used to make salt-baked chicken, a delicious chicken dish with a simple seasoning.

The Chinese are also famous for their grilled meats, especially grilled pork and grilled spareribs. For the best grilled meats, you have to grill on an open spit fired by charcoal. Alternatively, an electric grill or turbo broiler can be used.

IMPORTANT NOTES TO REMEMBER:

1. Choose the correct cut of meat.
2. Allow enough time for meat to marinate. When marinating large chunks of meat, prick with a fork so that the marinade can penetrate more effectively.
3. Always preheat the oven, grill or broiler before putting in the meat. The high heat will cook the outside of the meat very quickly and seal in the juices and flavour of the meat. Watch the timing carefully to prevent overcooking.
4. As the meat is cooking, brush with some melted fat to keep it moist. Put a pan below the meat to catch any drippings which can be used as a basting liquid or as a sauce.

SMOKING

Smoking adds fragrance and flavour to the meat. The meat is often partially cooked first by steaming, then cured in smoke from burning camphor wood, tea leaves or peanut shells. Smoking is usually done in a pot or a wok. Poultry is usually deep-fried after smoking to obtain the crispy skin, so well-loved by the Chinese.

COOKING UTENSILS

LADLES OR SPATULAS

The long ladle or spatula is best for cooking with the wok. When using an iron wok, you can use a metal spatula but a wooden spatula is needed when using a non-stick wok to prevent scratching.

CHOPPING BLOCK

The Chinese chopping block is usually round in shape, at least a few inches thick and quite heavy. Its heavy weight makes it ideal when chopping with a heavy cleaver, since the ingredients will not slip or move. After use, scrape the surface with the cleaver, brush with a wire mesh then wash and wipe dry. Never soak the chopping block in water. You should sun it occasionally to prevent an odour.

WOK

The wok is usually made of black cast iron or steel so it absorbs varying degrees of heat very quickly. Some woks are coated with non-stick material (Teflon) so they are easier to clean and reduce oil splatter from cooking. Flat bottomed woks are also available nowadays for cooking on electric plates. A wok cover can also be used to reduce cooking time and to prevent excessive reduction of liquid.

A wok should be seasoned properly before use. To season, wash the wok and dry it well then oil the surface by rubbing it with a little cooking oil. Heat up the wok then let it cool down. Repeat these steps for another 2–3 times, then wipe the wok with kitchen paper or cloth.

To clean the wok, place it under running water while it is still hot and brush off dirt. If using a non-stick wok, clean with a soft sponge instead. Avoid using harsh detergents to clean the wok. After cleaning, make sure that the wok is completely dry by wiping dry or heating up the wok.

CLAYPOT

Claypots are good for slow cooking methods such as braising and stewing because heat is absorbed and evenly distributed. There is also less evaporation as compared to other types of cooking pots and saucepans. As a result, meat, rice and porridge cooked in claypots taste more flavoursome.

After cooking, food can be served straight from the claypot. The food will be kept warm for a long time because the claypot can retain heat very well. Claypots are available in Chinese sundry shops and in a wide range of sizes.

CHINESE CLEAVER

The Chinese cleaver is used for chopping, cutting, slicing, mincing and shredding. Its flat side can also be used for crushing garlic.

Choose a good heavy cleaver made of carbon steel that will be suitable for most purposes. Sharpen with a whetstone regularly.

WIRE MESH LADLE

The Chinese wire mesh ladle with a wooden handle is usually used for scalding noodles. It is also useful for scooping up food during deep-frying. They are available in a variety of sizes but a 15-cm (6-in) diameter one should be appropriate for the home kitchen.

STEAMERS

Metal steamers are made up of a bottom section for holding water, a top section for placing perforated trays and a cover on top. Steam passes through the holes to cook the food. These steamers are readily available at Chinese sundry shops. A wok can also be used for steaming, as long as you have a tall cover and a steamer stand to hold the food above the water. For steaming breads and dumplings, bamboo steamers are used to prevent water from collecting and dripping onto the food.

When steaming food, remember to bring the water to the boil before putting in the food.

WEIGHTS & MEASURES

Quantities for this book are given in Metric, Imperial and American (spoon and cup) measures. Standard spoon and cup measurements used are: 1 tsp = 5 ml, 1 Tbsp = 15 ml, 1 cup = 250 ml. All measures are level unless otherwise stated.

Liquid And Volume Measures

Metric	Imperial	American
5 ml	$1/6$ fl oz	1 teaspoon
10 ml	$1/3$ fl oz	1 dessertspoon
15 ml	$1/2$ fl oz	1 tablespoon
60 ml	2 fl oz	$1/4$ cup (4 tablespoons)
85 ml	$2^1/2$ fl oz	$1/3$ cup
90 ml	3 fl oz	$3/8$ cup (6 tablespoons)
125 ml	4 fl oz	$1/2$ cup
180 ml	6 fl oz	$3/4$ cup
250 ml	8 fl oz	1 cup
300 ml	10 fl oz ($1/2$ pint)	$1^1/4$ cups
375 ml	12 fl oz	$1^1/2$ cups
435 ml	14 fl oz	$1^3/4$ cups
500 ml	16 fl oz	2 cups
625 ml	20 fl oz (1 pint)	$2^1/2$ cups
750 ml	24 fl oz ($1^1/5$ pints)	3 cups
1 litre	32 fl oz ($1^3/5$ pints)	4 cups
1.25 litres	40 fl oz (2 pints)	5 cups
1.5 litres	48 fl oz ($2^2/5$ pints)	6 cups
2.5 litres	80 fl oz (4 pints)	10 cups

Dry Measures

Metric	Imperial
30 grams	1 ounce
45 grams	$1^1/2$ ounces
55 grams	2 ounces
70 grams	$2^1/2$ ounces
85 grams	3 ounces
100 grams	$3^1/2$ ounces
110 grams	4 ounces
125 grams	$4^1/2$ ounces
140 grams	5 ounces
280 grams	10 ounces
450 grams	16 ounces (1 pound)
500 grams	1 pound, $1^1/2$ ounces
700 grams	$1^1/2$ pounds
800 grams	$1^3/4$ pounds
1 kilogram	2 pounds, 3 ounces
1.5 kilograms	3 pounds, $4^1/2$ ounces
2 kilograms	4 pounds, 6 ounces

Length

Metric	Imperial
0.5 cm	$1/4$ inch
1 cm	$1/2$ inch
1.5 cm	$3/4$ inch
2.5 cm	1 inch

Oven Temperature

	°C	°F	Gas Regulo
Very slow	120	250	1
Slow	150	300	2
Moderately slow	160	325	3
Moderate	180	350	4
Moderately hot	190/200	375/400	5/6
Hot	210/220	410/425	6/7
Very hot	230	450	8
Super hot	250/290	475/550	9/10

Abbreviation

tsp	teaspoon
Tbsp	tablespoon
g	gram
kg	kilogram
ml	millilitre

STARTERS

Fried Meat and Vegetable Dumplings

Deep-fried Pork Rolls

Steamed Mushrooms with Prawn Filling

Stuffed Capsicums (Bell Peppers)

Deep-fried Five-spice Rolls

FRIED MEAT AND VEGETABLE DUMPLINGS

Succulent meat and vegetable dumplings served with a vinegar and ginger dip.

Beat mixture against a bowl continuously for 1 minute to tenderise meat.

After shaping into a long roll, use a pastry cutter to divide dough into 18 equal pieces.

Pinch along the seam to seal dumpling into half-moon shape.

INGREDIENTS

Minced pork with a little fat	180 g (6 oz)
White cabbage (*pak choy*)	2 leaves, about 120 g (4 oz), finely chopped
Chinese chives	30 g (1 oz), finely chopped
Spring onion (scallion)	1, finely chopped
Cooking oil	2 Tbsp
Chicken stock (page 32)	185 ml (6 fl oz / $^3/_4$ cup)

SEASONING

Sugar	1 tsp
Salt	$^3/_4$ tsp
Ground white pepper	$^1/_4$ tsp
Light soy sauce	1 tsp
Chinese rice wine	1 tsp
Sesame oil	1 tsp
Cooked or shallot oil	1 Tbsp

DOUGH

Plain (all-purpose) flour	120 g (4 oz)
Salt	$^1/_4$ tsp
Boiling water	165 ml ($5^1/_3$ fl oz / $^2/_3$ cup)

VINEGAR AND GINGER DIP

Vinegar	2 Tbsp
Sugar	1 tsp
Ginger	30 g (1 oz), peeled and shredded

METHOD

- Prepare vinegar and ginger dip 1–2 hours ahead. Heat vinegar and sugar in a small pot until sugar dissolves. Pour immediately over ginger. Leave covered for 1–2 hours before serving.

- Combine ingredients for seasoning. Mix well with minced meat. Set aside.

- Place chopped cabbage in a muslin cloth and squeeze to remove excess vegetable liquid. Add to minced pork, with chives and spring onion. Mix to a smooth paste.

- Lift pork mixture with your hand and slap it against a bowl or chopping board continuously for 1 minute to improve texture of meat. Refrigerate meat mixture for 1 hour.

- To make dough, sift flour into a mixing bowl and add salt. Pour boiling water into flour and quickly mix into a stiff dough with a spoon. Form dough into a round ball and leave to rest, covered with a dry towel, for 30 minutes.

- Knead rested dough on a lightly floured board for 3–5 minutes until smooth. Shape into a long sausage roll and divide equally into 18 pieces.

- Make each piece into a round ball and roll out into a thin circle (about 7-cm / 3-in diameter).

- Put 1 tsp meat mixture, slightly off centre into each circle. Pleat one half of the wrapper and press against the unpleated side to seal and form a half-moon shape dumpling. Repeat until ingredients are used up.

- Heat a flat pan with 2 Tbsp oil until hot. Reduce heat and place dumplings in a circle close together. Fry for 1 minute until base of dumplings are golden brown. Do not move dumplings while frying.

- Pour chicken stock into pan, cover and simmer dumplings on low heat for 4–5 minutes until cooked through. Drain off remaining liquid and transfer dumplings onto a serving dish.

- Serve hot with vinegar and ginger dip.

DEEP-FRIED PORK ROLLS

Young bamboo shoots and Chinese mushrooms rolled in deep-fried pork make a tasty appetiser.

First slice meat without cutting through, then make next cut all the way through.

Place filling on flattened meat and roll up.

Heat the wok and deep-fry pork rolls for about 5 minutes or until golden.

INGREDIENTS

Boneless pork loin	250 g (9 oz), lightly frozen to facilitate slicing
Carrot	5-cm (2-in) piece, peeled and cut into strips
Canned bamboo shoots	5-cm (2-in) piece, cut into strips
Dried Chinese mushrooms	2 large pieces, soaked and shredded
Breadcrumbs	45 g (1^1/$_2$ oz)
Cooking oil	for deep-frying

SEASONING

Salt	^{1}/$_2$ tsp
Sugar	^{1}/$_2$ tsp
Ground white pepper	^{1}/$_4$ tsp
Chinese rice wine	2 tsp
Egg	1, beaten
Corn flour (cornstarch)	1 Tbsp

METHOD

- Double the size of the sliced meat so that it will be large enough to cover the vegetables. To do this, cut a 0.25-cm (^{1}/$_4$-in) thick slice across the grain without cutting through. Cut the next slice completely through 0.25-cm (^{1}/$_4$-in) from the first cut. Continue to do this with the whole piece of meat.

- Open up each slice of meat and beat lightly with the blunt edge of a cleaver to tenderise. Marinate meat with seasoning for 30 minutes.

- Open and spread out each piece of meat on a flat surface and place 2 strips each of carrot, bamboo shoots and dried mushrooms.

- Roll up meat, enclosing vegetables. Coat well with breadcrumbs.

- Heat oil for deep-frying in a wok. Deep-fry pork rolls for about 5 minutes or until golden. Drain well.

- Arrange pork rolls on a serving dish and garnish as desired.

STEAMED MUSHROOMS WITH PRAWN FILLING

Prawn-filled Chinese mushrooms served with a delicious chicken stock-based sauce.

Using a pair of kitchen scissors, remove stems from Chinese mushrooms.

Fill mushrooms with prawn mixture, then top with a pea and sliced sausage.

Pour leftover liquid from steaming into combined sauce B.

INGREDIENTS

Cooking oil	3 Tbsp
Dried Chinese mushrooms	12, soaked until soft and drained
Prawns (shrimps)	300 g (11 oz), shelled, deveined and minced
Water chestnuts	2, peeled and minced
Chinese sausage	1, sliced (optional)
Green peas	12
Egg white	$^1/_2$, beaten

SAUCE A (COMBINED)

Chicken stock (page 32)	250 ml (8 fl oz / 1 cup)
Salt	$^1/_2$ tsp
Ground white pepper	$^1/_2$ tsp
Sugar	$^1/_2$ tsp
Sesame oil	1 tsp
Oyster sauce	1 tsp

SEASONING

Salt	$^1/_4$ tsp
Ground white pepper	$^1/_4$ tsp
Sugar	$^1/_4$ tsp
Corn flour (cornstarch)	1 tsp
Sesame oil	$^1/_2$ tsp
Egg white	$^1/_2$, lightly beaten, to be added last (reserve half portion for the sauce)

SAUCE B (COMBINED)

Reserved mushroom stock	185 ml (6 fl oz / $^3/_4$ cup)
Chinese rice wine	1 tsp
Salt	$^1/_4$ tsp
Ground white pepper	$^1/_4$ tsp
Sugar	$^1/_4$ tsp
Corn flour (cornstarch)	1 tsp

METHOD

- Heat oil in a wok until hot. Stir-fry mushrooms for 1–2 minutes, then add combined sauce A and simmer for 5 minutes over low heat. Drain mushrooms from stock and allow to cool. Reserve stock for making sauce B.

- Combine minced prawns with water chestnuts and stir in seasoning ingredients. Add beaten egg white and beat with a spoon until mixture is sticky.

- Stuff mushrooms with prawn mixture and press a green pea and 1 or 2 slices of sausage on each of the stuffed mushrooms. Steam over rapidly boiling water for 10 minutes.

- Remove from steamer and carefully pour liquid into combined sauce B. Bring gravy to the boil. Reduce heat and simmer for 2–3 minutes. Add reserved beaten egg white and pour over mushrooms. Serve hot.

STUFFED CAPSICUMS (BELL PEPPERS)

If desired, you can use different coloured capsicums for a more colourful dish.

Cut around the stem of each capsicum. Remove the seeds and pith. Take care to keep capsicum whole.

Fill up each capsicum completely with the mixture.

Using a pair of tongs, carefully lower stuffed capsicum into hot oil to fry until slightly blistered.

INGREDIENTS

Dried prawns (shrimps)	1 1/2 Tbsp
Dried Chinese mushrooms	8, medium
Red capsicums (bell peppers)	4, large
Lean pork	175–200 g (6 1/2–7 oz)
Salt	1 1/2 tsp
Light soy sauce	2 Tbsp
Corn flour (cornstarch)	2 Tbsp
Vegetable oil	for deep-frying

SAUCE

Cooking oil	1 Tbsp
Chicken stock (page 32)	125 ml (4 fl oz / 1/2 cup)
Light soy sauce	2 Tbsp
Oyster sauce	4 Tbsp
Corn flour (cornstarch)	2 Tbsp, mixed with 3 Tbsp water

METHOD

- Soak dried prawns and mushrooms for 20 minutes in a bowl of warm water.

- Using a small knife, cut around the stem of each capsicum. Remove the cap, carefully, pulling out the seeds and any pith that comes with it. Be careful to keep capsicums whole.

- Finely chop the pork. Drain and chop prawns and mushrooms (discarding hard stems) and add to pork. Stir in salt and soy sauce. Stuff mixture in each capsicum through the hole, filling each one completely. Make a paste from corn flour mixed with 2 Tbsp water. Seal stuffing at the top of capsicums by spreading paste over the hole.

- Heat oil in a wok or deep-fat frier to 180°C (350°F); at this temperature a cube of stale bread will brown in 60 seconds. Lower capsicums, paste-side down, into the oil one by one. Turn the heat to low and fry capsicums for 3–4 minutes or until skins are softened and are slightly blistered.

- Remove capsicums from oil and drain well. Cut each capsicum into 4 pieces and arrange them in a heatproof dish. Stand dish on a rack in a steamer and bring the water beneath to the boil. Cover and steam steadily for 15 minutes.

- Meanwhile heat oil in a wok over medium-low heat and add the rest of sauce ingredients. Stir over high heat for 1–2 minutes until sauce thickens. Pour sauce over stuffed capsicums and serve immediately, from the heatproof dish.

DEEP-FRIED FIVE-SPICE ROLLS

This all-time favourite is usually served with ketchup, chilli sauce and soy-mustard dips.

Be careful when lifting bean curd sheets out after they have softened. Make sure you use both hands to spread them out and drain off water.

Shape filling into a sausage and place on bean curd sheet. Lift the edge of bean curd sheet to wrap over filling.

Roll up as tightly as possible. Use a pastry brush to apply some egg yolk on the edge to seal roll.

INGREDIENTS

Dried bean curd sheets	1 packet (225 g / 8 oz), 33 x 15-cm (13 x 6-in)
Pork with some fat in it	600 g (1 lb 5 oz), chopped into rice-sized bits
Spring onions (scallions)	12, the white part, cut into small rounds
Canned or fresh water chestnuts	175 g (6$^1/_2$ oz), peeled, chopped into rice-size bits
Tapioca flour or potato flour	3 Tbsp
Egg yolks	2, from medium-size eggs
Vegetable oil	for deep-frying
Thick dark soy sauce	1 Tbsp, mixed with 1 tsp prepared hot mustard to serve

MARINADE

Salt	1 tsp
Light soy sauce	2 tsp
Sugar	2$^1/_2$ tsp
Shao Hsing wine or medium-dry sherry	5 tsp
Sesame oil	2 tsp
Five-spice powder	1 tsp
Egg whites	1$^1/_2$, from medium-size eggs

METHOD

- Soak bean curd sheets in cold water for about 4 minutes or until sheets are soft and pliable. Lift each sheet carefully with both hands to drain, blot them with absorbent paper and place them flat on a large tea towel, one on top of another. Cover them with another tea towel to keep them just moist.

- Put finely chopped pork into a big bowl. Add ingredients for marinade, stir and leave for 5 minutes. Add spring onions and water chestnuts to mixture. Stir in tapioca flour or potato flour, 1 Tbsp at a time, to ensure smooth mixing. Divide mixture into 16 portions.

- Take a bean curd sheet from the covered pile and put it on a flat surface with the long side next to you. Cut sheet in half crossways.

- Scoop up a portion of filling and roll it between your palms into the shape of a sausage. Place filling near the edge of the bean curd sheet and roll it away from you as tightly as possible.

- Using either your fingers or a pastry brush, smear some egg yolk on the opposite edge and seal roll. Leave the two ends open like a cigarette and place roll on a tray, sealed side down. Cover tray with a damp cloth. Repeat until all the sheets are filled.

- If you are using a wok for deep-frying, half-fill it with vegetable oil. If you are using a deep-fat frier, the oil should be 6-cm (2^1/$_2$-in) deep. Heat oil to 190°C (375°F), at which temperature a cube of stale bread will brown in 50 seconds.

- Put in 8 rolls or however many will float freely in the oil. Deep-fry for 8 minutes or until golden brown in colour. Remove with a perforated ladle and drain on absorbent paper. Keep rolls warm. Repeat until all the rolls are done.

- Cut each roll into 5 pieces and put them on a large platter. Serve with soy-mustard dip or ketchup or chilli sauce.

SOUPS

Duck and Salted Vegetable Soup

Old Cucumber and Pork Soup

Bean Curd Hot Pot

Hot Sour Soup

Prawn Wantan Soup

DUCK AND SALTED VEGETABLE SOUP

A simple soup with duck and pickled plums.

Cut duck into 4 pieces for easy handling and cooking.

Squeeze out water from salted cabbage after soaking.

Add tomatoes with peppercorns and allow to simmer for another 10 minutes.

INGREDIENTS

Duck	$1/2$, about 1 kg (2 lb 3 oz)
Pickled mustard cabbage (*harm choy*)	250 g (9 oz), cut into 5-cm (2-in) squares
Cooking oil	1 Tbsp
Ginger	5-cm (2-in) knob, crushed
Water	2.5 litres (80 fl oz / 10 cups)
Pickled sour plums	2
Tomatoes	2, quartered
White peppercorns	$1/4$ tsp

METHOD

- Cut duck into 4 pieces and set aside.

- Soak pickled mustard cabbage in water for 1 hour. Drain and lightly squeeze out excess water.

- Heat oil in a pot and sauté ginger for 1–2 minutes until aromatic. Add duck and stir-fry for 5 minutes until duck changes colour.

- Pour water into the pot and add pickled mustard cabbage and sour plums. Bring to the boil, reduce heat to low, cover and simmer for $2^{1}/_{2}$ hours or until duck is tender.

- Add tomatoes and peppercorns and simmer for a further 10 minutes.

- Serve hot.

OLD CUCUMBER AND PORK SOUP

A refreshing clear soup with a definite crunch to it.

Use a spoon to scoop out all the seeds from the old cucumber.

Add the ingredients to the pot, then cover and bring to boil before seasoning with salt.

While soup is simmering, make sure to skim off any surface scum as it accumulates.

INGREDIENTS

Old cucumber with skin	1, large
Lean pork with some fat	360 g (12 oz), whole piece, uncut and rinsed
Dried Chinese red dates	6, seeded and rinsed
Water	1.25 litres (40 fl oz / 5 cups)
Salt	1 1/2 tsp
Light soy sauce	2 Tbsp

METHOD

- Cut old cucumber in half lengthways. Scoop out seeds with a spoon and cut each half into 5-cm (2-in) pieces.

- Place cucumber, pork, red dates and water in a large pot. Cover and bring to the boil.

- Add salt, reduce heat and simmer for 45–60 minutes. Skim off surface scum from time to time.

- When pork is tender, remove and cut into 2-cm (1-in) thick slices. Return pork to soup.

- Serve soup with a small dish of light soy sauce as a dip for the pork.

BEAN CURD HOT POT

This popular Chinese soup is made with minced chicken, bean curd and bamboo shoots.

Use a spoon to press bean curd through a sieve to make into a paste.

Pour egg yolk mixture into bean curd and chicken mixture. Mix until well combined.

Cover, then steam mixture over high heat for 7 minutes.

INGREDIENTS

Soft bean curd	6 pieces or 6 packets silken bean curd
Chicken	60 g (2 oz), minced
Egg yolks	3
Salt	to taste
Ground white pepper	to taste
Cooking oil	2 tsp
Tender tips of winter bamboo shoot	30 g (1 oz)
Salt	to taste
Lettuce leaves	3–4

CHICKEN STOCK

Chicken bones	2 kg (2 lb 3 oz), skin and fat discarded
Water	2 litres (64 fl oz / 8 cups)

METHOD

- Prepare chicken stock. Rinse bones until water is clear. Place into a stockpot and add water. Bring to the boil over high heat. Boil for 1–2 hours skimming off scum that surfaces from time to time. Strain to get about 1.5 litres (48 fl oz / 5 cups) stock.

- Pass bean curd through a sieve. Mix with minced chicken.

- Beat egg yolks with salt and pepper. Add to bean curd and chicken mixture and blend well.

- Pour mixture into a mould lightly greased with cooking oil. Steam over high heat for 7 minutes before serving.

- Meanwhile, reheat chicken stock and add bamboo shoot. Boil for 10 minutes. Season to taste with salt.

- Put steamed bean curd mixture into a big soup bowl and pour boiling stock over. Add lettuce leaves, garnish and serve immediately.

HOT SOUR SOUP

Chicken and prawns add flavour to this peppery chicken stock-based soup.

Cut bean curd into small cubes.

After adding in green peas, allow to simmer for another 5 minutes.

Add in lightly beaten eggs as a final step.

INGREDIENTS

Chicken drumstick	1, boned and cut into small cubes
Small shelled prawns (shrimps) (optional)	300 g (11 oz), diced
Chicken stock (page 32)	2.25 litres (9 cups)
Sichuan vegetable	1 large piece, unwashed and diced
Carrot	1, peeled and diced
Dried Chinese mushrooms	4, soaked and diced
Button mushrooms	$1/2$ can, halved
Straw mushrooms	$1/2$ can, halved
Fresh baby corn	10 cobs, diced
Red chillies	3, split to remove seeds
Chinese black vinegar	165 ml ($5^{1}/_{3}$ fl oz / $^{2}/_{3}$ cup)
Soft bean curd	1 square piece, diced
Frozen green peas	100 g ($3^{1}/_{2}$ oz), rinsed
Sweet potato flour	4 Tbsp, mixed with 125 ml (4 fl oz / $^{1}/_{2}$ cup) chicken stock, strained
Eggs	2, lightly beaten

SEASONING

Ground white pepper	1 tsp
Salt	1 tsp
Corn flour (cornstarch)	1 tsp

METHOD

- Marinate chicken and prawns with seasoning ingredients for 15 minutes.

- Pour strained stock into a deep cooking pot and bring to the boil. Add Sichuan vegetable, carrot, all the mushrooms, corn, chillies and black vinegar. Allow to simmer for 10 minutes.

- Add chicken and prawns and when mixture begins to boil, add bean curd and green peas. Simmer for another 5 minutes, then stir in strained sweet potato flour mixture and finally the beaten eggs.

- Serve hot.

PRAWN WANTAN SOUP

Prawn dumplings add a wonderful flavour to this clear soup.

Place 1 tsp filling in the centre of a wantan wrapper.

Wrap around filling and gather edges together. Press firmly to seal.

Pour stock over wantans and vegetables, then serve with chopped spring onion as garnish.

INGREDIENTS

Small shelled prawns (shrimps)	150 g (5 oz), minced
Pork	120 g (4 oz), minced
Fresh water chestnuts	3, peeled and finely minced
Dried Chinese mushrooms	2, soaked and finely minced
Egg white	$1/2$, beaten
Wantan wrappers	120 g (4 oz)
Cooking oil	1 Tbsp
Chinese flowering cabbage (*choy sum*)	2 stalks, cut into 3 sections
Spring onions (scallions)	2, chopped

SEASONING INGREDIENTS

Light soy sauce	1 tsp
Salt	$1/2$ tsp
Sugar	$1/2$ tsp
Ground white pepper	$1/4$ tsp
Corn flour (cornstarch)	1 tsp

STOCK

Chicken stock (page 32)	1.5 litres (48 fl oz / 6 cups)
Salt	$1 1/2$ tsp
Sesame oil	1 tsp
Ground white pepper	$1/2$ tsp

METHOD

- Mix prawns, pork, water chestnuts and mushrooms with egg white and seasoning ingredients and leave for 30 minutes.

- Put 1 tsp mixture in the centre of each wantan wrapper. Wrap around filling and fold edges to seal.

- Boil a saucepan of water and add 1 Tbsp oil. Drop wantans in boiling water and cook for 1 minute. Remove with a perforated ladle and place in a deep soup bowl. Scald vegetables in the same boiling water for 1 minute. Drain and arrange around the sides of the bowl.

- Bring stock ingredients to the boil. Pour over wantans and vegetables. Serve garnished with chopped spring onion.

SEAFOOD

Stir-fried Sichuan Style Squid

Chilli Oyster Crabs

Sea Bass with Spicy Black Vinegar Sauce

Butter Prawns with Toasted Coconut

Crab Omelette

Fried Oyster Fritters

Braised Fish with Black Bean Sauce

Claypot Fish Head

STIR-FRIED SICHUAN STYLE SQUID

Large fresh squid stir-fried with hot bean paste, celery and chilli.

Carefully score the inside of squid body, taking care not to cut through completely.

Stir-fry garlic and hot bean paste in a wok until fragrant. Then add in celery and stir-fry.

To coat squid evenly with sauce, lightly stir and turn ingredients in wok. Do not overcook squid or it will be tough.

INGREDIENTS

Fresh large squid	600 g (1 lb 4 oz), cleaned, inner body scored, then cut into thick slices, about 2 x 5-cm (1 x 2-in)
Salt	1/2 tsp
Ground white pepper	1/2 tsp
Cooking oil	3 Tbsp
Garlic	3 cloves, peeled and minced
Hot bean paste	1 Tbsp
Tender young celery	1 stalk, sliced
Red chillies	2, seeded and sliced

SAUCE (COMBINED)

Chicken stock (page 32) or water	375 ml (12 fl oz / 1 1/2 cups)
Light soy sauce	1 Tbsp
Chinese wine	1 Tbsp
Sesame oil	1 tsp
Sugar	1 tsp
Ground white pepper	1/4 tsp
Salt	1/4 tsp
Corn flour (cornstarch)	2 tsp

METHOD

- Season squid with salt and pepper for 15 minutes. Blanch seasoned squid in boiling salted water for 30–60 seconds. Drain well.

- Heat wok with oil until hot and stir-fry garlic and hot bean paste until fragrant. Add celery and stir-fry for 1 1/2 minutes.

- Stir in sauce ingredients and bring to the boil. When sauce thickens, add squid and chillies, and very briefly toss mixture.

- Transfer to a serving dish. Garnish and serve hot.

CHILLI OYSTER CRABS

Delicious chill crabs given a twist with oyster sauce and Chinese wine.

When cleaning crabs, remove pincers and crack shell open with a nutcracker.

Add crabs to wok and stir with chillies, ginger, garlic and shallots.

When crabs turn to bright red in colour, add in lightly beaten eggs.

INGREDIENTS

Crabs	3 kg (6 lb 9 oz)
Cooking oil	250 ml (8 fl oz / 1 cup)
Ginger	60 g (2 oz), peeled and cut into strips
Garlic	7 cloves, peeled and sliced
Shallots	7, peeled and sliced
Red chillies	10, seeded, machine blended with 125 ml (4 fl oz / $^1/_2$ cup) water
Eggs	5, beaten lightly
Spring onions (scallions)	6, cut into 5-cm (2-in) lengths
Coriander leaves (cilantro)	2 sprigs, cut into 5-cm (2-in) lengths

SAUCE

Chinese rice wine	3 Tbsp
Chilli sauce	3 Tbsp
Oyster sauce	4 Tbsp
Sugar	4 tsp
Sesame oil	1 tsp
Ground white pepper	$^1/_4$ tsp

METHOD

- Clean crabs, remove and crack pincers with a crab cracker. Trim legs and cut into 4 pieces.

- Heat oil in a large wok and stir-fry ginger, garlic and shallots until fragrant. Put in chillies and fry for 2 minutes.

- Add crabs and stir briskly. Cover wok for approximately 4–5 minutes. Uncover and stir briskly once again, then add sauce ingredients. When crabs are bright red and nearly cooked, pour in beaten eggs. Add spring onions, stirring to mix with sauce.

- Dish out, garnish with coriander leaves and serve hot with rice or toasted bread.

SEA BASS WITH SPICY BLACK VINEGAR SAUCE

Fried sea bass served with black vinegar sauce and a dash of chilli.

Cut a criss-cross pattern on fish to help it cook faster.

Fry fish, then turn and fry on the other side, until batter is golden brown.

Pour thickened sauce over fish just before serving.

INGREDIENTS

Sea bass or any freshwater fish	500–600 g (1 lb 1 1/2 oz–1 lb 5 oz)
Salt	1 tsp
Ground white pepper	1/2 tsp
Corn flour (cornstarch)	for coating fish
Cooking oil	5 Tbsp
Garlic	2 large cloves, peeled and thinly sliced
Ginger	2.5-cm (1-in) knob, peeled and thinly sliced
Red chilli	1, sliced
Spring onions (scallions)	2
Corn flour (cornstarch)	2 tsp, mixed with 2 Tbsp chicken stock or water

SAUCE (COMBINED)

Chicken stock (page 32)	165 ml (5 1/3 fl oz / 2/3 cup)
Light soy sauce	3/4 Tbsp
Dark soy sauce	1/4 tsp
Sugar	60 g
Black vinegar	2 Tbsp
Salt	a pinch

METHOD

- Use a sharp knife and deeply score both sides of the fish, starting about 4-cm (1 1/2-in) from gill opening. Lightly cut a criss-cross pattern on tail end.

- Marinate fish with salt and pepper and set aside for 15 minutes. Coat fish with corn flour, making sure to coat the slits.

- Heat 3 Tbsp oil in a non-stick frying pan and fry fish on both sides, covered, until batter is crisp and golden brown (about 10 minutes). Place fish on serving dish.

- Reheat pan with 2 Tbsp cooking oil. Add garlic and ginger and stir-fry for 20 seconds until fragrant. Stir in chilli and combined sauce ingredients and bring to a rapid boil.

- Add spring onions. Thicken with corn flour mixture and pour sauce over fish. Serve hot.

BUTTER PRAWNS WITH TOASTED COCONUT

Buttered shrimps tossed with toasted coconut is an unmistakably luscious dish.

Use a pair of kitchen scissors to snip off the feelers of large prawns.

Swirl beaten egg around in the frying pan to make a thin omelette.

Add toasted coconut, sugar, salt and bird's eye chillies to heated butter and cook until fragrant.

INGREDIENTS

Large prawns (shrimps)	500 g (1 lb 1^1/$_2$ oz), feelers trimmed
Salt	1 tsp
Ground white pepper	^{1}/$_2$ tsp
Cooking oil	as needed
Butter	90 g (3 oz)
Pan-toasted grated coconut	60 g (2 oz), blended in electric blender
Sugar	2 tsp
Bird's eye chillies	10, finely sliced
Chopped spring onion (scallion) and coriander (cilantro) leaves	
Small lime	1, juice extracted

OMELETTE

Eggs	2, beaten
Light soy sauce	1 tsp
Salt	^{1}/$_4$ tsp
Ground white pepper	^{1}/$_2$ tsp

METHOD

- Season prawns with ^{1}/$_2$ tsp salt and pepper for 30 minutes.

- Combine ingredients for omelette. Heat a non-stick frying pan and add ^{1}/$_2$ Tbsp oil. Pour in beaten egg and swirl pan around to make a thin omelette. When omelette is set, remove from pan and leave to cool.

- Roll cooled omelette up and slice finely.

- Heat 3 Tbsp oil in a wok. Fry seasoned prawns until just cooked. Prawns are cooked when they turn pink. Drain from oil.

- Heat butter in a clean wok over low heat. Add toasted coconut, sugar, ^{1}/$_2$ tsp salt and bird's eye chillies. Toss well until fragrant.

- Add chopped omelette, spring onion, coriander leaves and lime juice to wok. Stir to mix, then dish out and serve immediately.

CRAB OMELETTE

An exotic and tasty omelette is delightful when served on a bed of deep-fried vermicelli.

When oil is smoking hot, deep-fry vermicelli until puffed and crisp. This takes about 2 seconds.

Fry crabmeat mixture for 10 seconds, then drain with a perforated ladle.

Add rice wine after frying mixture briskly.

INGREDIENTS

Crabmeat	350 g (12 oz)
Rice vermicelli	120 g (4 oz)
Cooking oil	800 ml (26^2/$_3$ fl oz / 3^1/$_4$ cups)
Egg whites	6
Winter bamboo shoots	360 g (12 oz), shredded
Corn flour (cornstarch)	1^1/$_2$ Tbsp
Chicken stock (page 32) or water	4 Tbsp
Sesame oil	^{1}/$_4$ tsp
Salt	^{1}/$_2$ tsp
Rice wine	1 tsp

METHOD

- Fry rice vermicelli in boiling oil for 2 seconds. Drain. Vermicelli should be white and crisp. (Do not wash vermicelli, use it straight from the packet for best results.) Reserve oil.

- Beat egg whites until stiff and mix it in a big bowl with crabmeat, bamboo shoots, half the corn flour, chicken stock or water, sesame oil and salt.

- Reheat oil until it boils. Fry mixture for 10 seconds. Drain. Return dry mixture to pan and fry briskly. Add rice wine.

- Mix remaining corn flour with 2 Tbsp water. Add to crabmeat to thicken it.

- Line a plate with crisp rice vermicelli and pour crab mixture on top just before serving.

FRIED OYSTER FRITTERS

A delightful dish of deep-fried oysters served with tomato sauce.

INGREDIENTS

Oysters	450 g (1 lb), shucked
Self-raising flour	50 g (1¹/₄ oz)
Plain (all-purpose) flour	110 g (4 oz)
Eggs	3, beaten lightly
Water	4 Tbsp
Ground white pepper	a pinch
Salt	a pinch
Cooking oil	2 Tbsp
Parsley	8 sprigs, broken into small sections
Tomato sauce	for serving

METHOD

- Rinse oysters in a basin of salted water, then rinse in fresh water twice.

- Mix self-raising flour, plain flour and eggs together. Add water, pepper and salt. Blend well to form a smooth batter. Add oysters to batter.

- Heat oil in a frying pan. Drop battered oyster into frying pan a tablespoonful at a time and cook until golden brown. Remove with a perforated ladle.

- Garnish with small sprigs of parsley. Serve with tomato sauce.

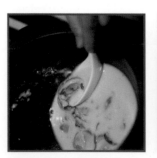

Scoop out a spoonful of mixture with an oyster.

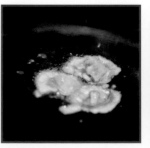

Drop the spoonful of mixture into a pan of hot oil and fry until it turns golden brown.

When cooked, remove from hot oil and drain with a perforated ladle.

BRAISED FISH WITH BLACK BEAN SAUCE

Deep-fried whole fish braised in a light anchovy stock-based sauce.

Coat whole fish with corn flour just before deep-frying.

Add chillies and sauce ingredients to stir-fried black beans, shallots, garlic and ginger.

Lower deep-fried fish gently into the wok. Reduce the heat a little and cover, allowing it to simmer until cooked.

INGREDIENTS

Whole fish (garoupa, threadfin, red snapper)	1, about 1 kg (2 lb 3 oz)
Cooking oil	for deep-frying
Shallots	2, peeled and sliced
Garlic	2 cloves, peeled and minced
Ginger	5 slices, peeled and minced
Fermented black beans	1 Tbsp, soaked in water for 10 minutes, drained and minced
Red chillies	2, chopped
Corn flour (cornstarch)	2 tsp, mixed with 2 Tbsp water
Spring onions (scallions)	2, chopped

SEASONING

Salt	$1/2$ tsp
Ground white pepper	$1/2$ tsp
Light soy sauce	2 tsp
Chinese rice wine	1 Tbsp
Egg white	1, beaten
Corn flour (cornstarch)	1 Tbsp, to be added just before frying fish

SAUCE (COMBINED)

Fresh anchovy stock	250 ml (8 fl oz / 1 cup)
Light soy sauce	2 tsp
Dark soy sauce	$1/2$ tsp
Chinese rice wine	2 tsp
Black vinegar	1 tsp
Sugar	$1 1/2$ tsp
Salt	$1/4$ tsp
Ground white pepper	$1/4$ tsp

METHOD

- Clean and scale fish. Cut two deep slits 2.5-cm (1-in) apart across each side of the body. Season fish with seasoning ingredients for at least 30 minutes. Just before deep-frying fish, coat with corn flour.

- Heat oil in a wok until hot. Fry fish for 2–3 minutes on each side. Remove and drain from oil.

- Reheat a clean wok with 2 Tbsp oil and stir-fry shallots, garlic and ginger until fragrant. Add fermented black beans and stir-fry until aromatic. Put in chillies and sauce ingredients.

- Return fish to the wok and reduce heat a little. Cover the wok and allow to simmer for 3–5 minutes, or until fish is cooked. Remove fish carefully and place on a serving dish.

- Thicken sauce with corn flour mixture and add spring onions. Pour sauce over fish and serve hot.

CLAYPOT FISH HEAD

Crunchy fish head served with a sweet and tangy sauce in a claypot.

Add fish head pieces to batter and turn to coat completely. Deep-fry fish head pieces in hot oil until golden brown.

Heat 3 Tbsp oil in the claypot. Add ginger and onion and sauté until fragrant.

Add fried fish head pieces to claypot. Then add bean curd cubes and cover to simmer for 5–8 minutes.

INGREDIENTS

Fish head (garoupa, threadfin, red snapper)	1, about 800 g (1³/₄ lb), chopped into large pieces
Chinese rice wine	¹/₂ Tbsp
Light soy sauce	¹/₂ Tbsp
Ginger juice	¹/₂ Tbsp
Ground white pepper	¹/₂ tsp
Cooking oil	for deep-frying + 3 Tbsp
Soft bean curd	1 square piece, cut into 2.5-cm (1-in) cubes
Ginger	2.5-cm (1-in) knob, peeled and sliced
Onion	1, peeled and cut into 6 wedges
Dried Chinese mushrooms	4
Canned button mushrooms	6–8
Red chillies	2, sliced
Spring onions (scallions)	2, cut into 2.5-cm (1 in) sections
Corn flour (cornstarch)	¹/₂ Tbsp, mixed with 1 Tbsp water
Lettuce leaves	6–8, washed

BATTER

Egg	1, beaten
Corn flour (cornstarch)	2 Tbsp
Water	2 Tbsp

SAUCE

Chicken stock (page 32)	250 ml (8 fl oz / 1 cup)
Oyster sauce	1 Tbsp
Light soy sauce	¹/₂ Tbsp
Chinese rice wine	2 tsp
Sesame oil	1 tsp
Sugar	1 tsp
Ground white pepper	¹/₂ tsp

METHOD

- Clean fish head and marinate with rice wine, soy sauce, ginger juice and pepper for 30 minutes.

- Heat wok with oil for deep-frying until hot. Coat fish head with batter and deep-fry fish head for 5–8 minutes on each side until golden brown and cooked. Set aside.

- Put in bean curd and deep-fry for 2 minutes. Drain from oil and leave aside.

- Heat claypot with 3 Tbsp cooking oil and sauté ginger and onion until fragrant.

- Put in mushrooms and stir-fry for 1 minute. Add button mushrooms and chillies and toss briskly.

- Pour in combined sauce ingredients and bring to the boil.

- Put in fish head and bean curd. Reduce heat a little, cover and simmer for 5–8 minutes. Add spring onions and thicken with corn flour mixture.

- Arrange lettuce leaves around sides of claypot and serve immediately.

MEAT &
POULTRY

Beef Patties in Tomato Sauce

Chicken Stew with Fresh Chestnuts

Fried Garlic Pork

Five-spice Crispy Skin Chicken

Pig's Trotters in Chinese Black Vinegar

Ginger Chicken in Earthen Pot

Teochew Duck

Roast Pork Ribs

BEEF PATTIES IN TOMATO SAUCE

Tasty beef patties shallow-fried and cooked in tomato sauce.

INGREDIENTS

Minced beef	450 g (1 lb)
Green (mung) bean flour	2 Tbsp
Ground white pepper	a pinch
Salt	$^1/_2$ tsp
Cooking oil	6 Tbsp
Light soy sauce	1 Tbsp
Water	425 ml (14 fl oz / 1$^3/_4$ cups)
Tomato sauce	2 Tbsp
Sugar	a pinch
Tomatoes	5, quartered
Worcestershire sauce	$^1/_2$ Tbsp

METHOD

- Season beef with flour, pepper and salt. Shape into patties.

- Heat oil in a pan over medium heat and fry beef patties until golden brown. This will take about 5 minutes.

- Pour soy sauce, water and tomato sauce over patties. Simmer for 30 minutes over very low heat. Add sugar and tomatoes. Add Worcestershire sauce just before serving.

After mixing beef with flour, pepper and salt, shape into balls and flatten into patties.

Fry patties in a frying pan, turning over to cook both sides.

Add tomato quarters into frying pan after adding sugar.

CHICKEN STEW WITH FRESH CHESTNUTS

Chunky chicken pieces stewed in rice wine with mushrooms and fresh chestnuts.

INGREDIENTS

Chicken	1, about 1.75 kg (3 lb 13$^1/_2$ oz)
Light soy sauce	$^1/_2$ tsp
Chestnuts	675 g (1 lb 6$^1/_2$ oz)
Garlic	6 cloves, peeled
Preserved soy beans	2 Tbsp
Dried Chinese mushrooms	6, soaked, stems removed and cut into strips
Cooking oil	4 Tbsp
Rice wine	1$^1/_2$ Tbsp
Water	800 ml (28 fl oz / 3$^1/_2$ cups)
Brown sugar	a pinch
Salt	$^1/_2$ tsp
Green (mung) bean flour	1 Tbsp, mixed with 1 Tbsp water

METHOD

- Rub chicken with soy sauce. Dip chestnuts in boiling water for 2 seconds, remove and leave in cold water for 3 minutes. Shell and remove hairy membrane. Pound garlic to a paste with preserved soy beans.

- Heat oil in a wok over medium heat and fry pounded garlic and soy bean mixture for 3 minutes. Add chicken and turn briskly several times. Increase heat to brown chicken. Add rice wine, water, chestnuts, mushrooms, brown sugar and salt. Cover tightly and bring to the boil. Reduce heat and stew for 1 hour.

- Remove chicken to a chopping board and cut into large pieces. Arrange onto serving plate. Add flour paste to gravy in the wok and bring to the boil. Pour hot gravy over chicken. Arrange chestnuts around chicken and place mushrooms on top.

After treating chestnuts with hot and cold water, it will be easier to remove the shell and membrane.

Place peeled garlic and preserved soy beans in a mortar and pound to a paste.

After chopping up chicken, arrange pieces on a serving plate to form the shape of a whole chicken.

FRIED GARLIC PORK

Thin slices of pork stir-fried in hot chilli and garlic sauce.

Place seasoning ingredients in a mixing bowl and add pork to marinate for 30 minutes.

Add pork pieces to hot oil to deep-fry and stir lightly with a pair of long chopsticks to separate the pieces.

Stir-fry fried pork pieces in the combined sauce ingredients until sauce thickens.

INGREDIENTS

Pork fillet or tender cut	500 g (1 lb 1 1/2 oz), thinly sliced
Cooking oil	for deep-frying
Chilli oil	1 Tbsp
Garlic	10–12 cloves, peeled and sliced
Coriander leaves (cilantro)	2 sprigs for garnishing

SEASONING INGREDIENTS

Light soy sauce	1/2 Tbsp
Five-spice powder	a pinch
Black peppercorns	1 tsp, lightly crushed
Corn flour (cornstarch)	2 tsp
Cooking oil	1 Tbsp, to be added just before cooking

SAUCE INGREDIENTS (COMBINED)

Light soy sauce	1/2 Tbsp
Oyster sauce	1 tsp
Dark soy sauce	1/2 tsp
Sugar	1/2 tsp

METHOD

- Marinate pork with seasoning ingredients for 30 minutes. Just before cooking, add 1 Tbsp oil to the meat to prevent sticking.

- Heat oil fin a large wok and stir-fry pork for 1 minute. Drain well and set aside.

- Remove oil from the wok. Heat chilli oil and lightly brown garlic.

- Pour in combined sauce ingredients, then add fried pork and stir-fry for 2 minutes until sauce thickens.

- Dish onto a serving plate and garnish with coriander leaves.

FIVE-SPICE CRISPY SKIN CHICKEN

Crispy cornflake-coated chicken served with lettuce and cucumber.

Combine flour coating mixture ingredients in a mixing bowl. Place chicken pieces in mixture and turn to coat completely.

Dip chicken pieces into batter and deep-fry in hot oil until golden brown.

Scoop out chicken pieces and drain well with a perforated ladle.

INGREDIENTS

Chicken	1, about 1 kg (2 lb 3 oz) or 4 chicken thighs, cut into large pieces
Cooking oil	for deep-frying
Lettuce and cucumber slices	

SEASONING

Sugar	1 Tbsp
Salt	1 tsp
Ground white pepper	1 tsp
Five-spice powder	$^1/_2$ tsp
Egg	1, lightly beaten
Water	2 Tbsp
Self-raising flour	2 Tbsp

FLOUR COATING MIXTURE (COMBINED)

Cornflakes	60 g (2 oz), finely ground
Self-raising flour	240 g (8 oz)
Salt	$^1/_2$ tsp
Ground white pepper	$^1/_2$ tsp
Bicarbonate of soda	$^1/_4$ tsp

BATTER

Self-raising flour	60 g (2 oz)
Water or milk	185 ml (6 fl oz / $^3/_4$ cup)
Salt	$^1/_4$ tsp
Ground white pepper	$^1/_4$ tsp

METHOD

- Marinate chicken with seasoning ingredients for 1–2 hours.

- Heat oil in a large wok. Just before frying, coat chicken pieces with flour coating mixture. Dip into batter mixture and drop into hot oil. Fry over high heat for 1 minute, then reduce heat to moderate and cook until chicken turns golden-brown.

- Drain well and serve with lettuce or cucumber slices.

PIG'S TROTTERS IN CHINESE BLACK VINEGAR

A delicious dish of fried pig's trotters simmered in black vinegar.

Scald trotters in boiling water for 5 minutes and drain well with a perforated ladle.

Stir-fry ground ingredients in a claypot until fragrant.

Pour in vinegar, sugar and enough water to cover all the trotters.

INGREDIENTS

Pig's trotters	2, cleaned and cut into 5-cm (2-in) pieces
Cooking oil	3 Tbsp
Soy bean paste	5 tsp, ground
Chinese black vinegar	5 tsp
Sugar	2 tsp
Water	1.5 litres (48 fl oz / 6 cups) or enough to cover trotters
Dark soy sauce	1 tsp

GROUND INGREDIENTS

Shallots	15, peeled
Garlic	15 cloves, peeled
Red chillies	6

METHOD

- Boil a large pot of water and scald trotters for 5 minutes. Drain and set aside.

- Heat oil in a deep claypot and stir-fry ground ingredients until fragrant. Add ground soy bean paste and continue to stir-fry until fragrant. Add trotters and fry for another 3 minutes. If necessary, sprinkle with a little water to prevent burning. Add vinegar, sugar and enough water to cover trotters.

- Cover claypot and bring to the boil. Reduce heat and allow to simmer for 1¹/₂ hours until trotters are tender, stirring occasionally to prevent sticking. Stir in dark soy sauce just before serving.

GINGER CHICKEN IN EARTHEN POT

Bite-sized chicken pieces cooked with mushrooms, carrots and bamboo shoots in a claypot.

Peel ginger and wipe it clean with a damp cloth. Cut into slices.

Place bean curd slices into oil one by one to prevent them from sticking to one another.

Add vegetables to the claypot and stir lightly to ensure that the ingredients are well mixed.

INGREDIENTS

Chicken	1, about 1 kg (2 lb 3 oz), cut into bite-size pieces
Cooking oil	for deep-frying + 2 Tbsp
Firm bean curd	4 small squares, sliced into 1 x 2.5-cm (¹/₂ x 1-in) pieces
Ginger	6 slices, peeled
Garlic	4 cloves, peeled and sliced
Shallots	4, peeled and sliced
Dried Chinese mushrooms	5, soaked and halved
Carrots	120 g (4 oz), peeled and sliced
Canned bamboo shoots	90 g (3 oz), sliced
Tientsin cabbage	240 g (8 oz), cut into 5-cm (2-in) lengths
Red chillies	2, sliced
Spring onions (scallions)	6, cut into 2.5-cm (1-in) lengths

SEASONING INGREDIENTS

Salt	1 tsp
Sugar	1 tsp
Dark soy sauce	1 tsp
Light soy sauce	2 tsp
Corn flour (cornstarch)	1 Tbsp

SAUCE INGREDIENTS (COMBINED)

Chicken stock (page 32)	375 ml (12 fl oz / 1¹/₂ cups)
Salt	¹/₂ tsp
Sugar	1 tsp
Ground white pepper	¹/₂ tsp
Light soy sauce	1 Tbsp
Oyster sauce	1 Tbsp
Dark soy sauce	1 tsp
Sesame oil	1 tsp

METHOD

- Marinate chicken with seasoning ingredients for 20 minutes.

- Heat oil in a wok and deep-fry bean curd pieces until golden brown. Remove and set aside. Deep-fry chicken for 5 minutes. Drain and place in a claypot. Reserve seasoning ingredients for later use.

- Reheat a clean wok with 2 Tbsp oil and lightly brown ginger, garlic and shallots. Add mushrooms and stir-fry until fragrant. Add carrots, bamboo shoots and *Tientsin* cabbage and fry for 3–5 minutes. Combine ingredients for sauce and stir well. Add to wok and bring to the boil.

- Pour sauce over chicken in claypot, add chillies and when it boils again, reduce heat, cover and simmer for 25 minutes or until chicken is tender.

- Add bean curd pieces and spring onions, and simmer for another 5–10 minutes.

- Thicken sauce with reserved seasoning mixture and serve.

TEOCHEW DUCK

Deep-fried duck simmered in light soy sauce and served with hard-boiled eggs.

Place duck on a flat surface. Rub duck all over, including the inside, with salt and five-spice powder.

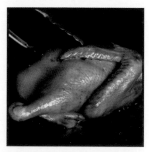

Using a pair of tongs, fry duck in hot oil until lightly browned.

With a sharp knife, cut duck into slices for serving.

INGREDIENTS

Duck	1, about 1.5 kg (3 lb 4¹/₂ oz)
Salt	1 tsp
Five-spice powder	1 tsp
Galangal	120 g (4 oz), peeled and sliced
Cooking oil	for deep-frying
Sugar	2 Tbsp
Dark soy sauce	2 Tbsp
Water	1.25 litres (40 fl oz / 5 cups) or enough to cover more than half the duck
Light soy sauce	1 Tbsp
Hard-boiled eggs	6, shelled
Coriander leaves (cilantro)	for garnishing

METHOD

- Rub inside and outside of duck with salt and five-spice powder. Stuff duck with galangal slices, keeping 3 slices aside. Let duck stand for at least 2 hours.

- Heat oil in a deep wok until hot and fry duck for 5 minutes until lightly browned. Remove and drain well. Pour away oil, leaving 2 Tbsp in the wok and add sugar and the remaining galangal slices. When oil turns dark, turn off heat. Add dark soy sauce. Return duck to wok and coat the whole duck with sauce.

- Pour water to cover more than half of the duck. Put in light soy sauce and hard-boiled eggs. Bring to the boil, then cover and simmer for about 20 minutes. Remove eggs and set aside.

- Turn duck and continue to simmer over low heat for about 1¹/₂–2 hours, until duck is tender and sauce is thick. Turn duck occasionally while simmering.

- To serve, slice duck and halve eggs. Arrange onto serving dish and pour sauce over. Garnish with coriander leaves.

ROAST PORK RIBS

Pork ribs marinated in garlic and ginger and roasted over a slow fire.

When ribs are roasting on the wire rack, baste them with marinade occasionally and turn them over every 15 minutes.

Add maltose to the remaining portion of marinade and cook over low heat.

Dip ribs into maltose mixture to coat completely. Then grill until well roasted.

INGREDIENTS

Pork ribs	1.2 kg (2 lb 12 oz), kept in whole panels about 10–12-cm (4–5-in) long
Garlic	4 cloves, peeled and finely chopped
Ginger	2 thin slices, peeled
Star anise	1 piece
Maltose	1 Tbsp

SEASONING INGREDIENTS

Coarse sugar	120 g (4 oz)
Light soy sauce	3 Tbsp
Dark soy sauce	1 tsp
Oyster sauce	2 Tbsp
Hoisin sauce	1 $^1/_2$ Tbsp
Plum sauce	1 $^1/_2$ Tbsp
Chinese rice wine	1 Tbsp
Ginger powder	$^1/_2$ tsp
Five-spice powder	1 tsp
Sesame oil	1 Tbsp
Ground white pepper	$^1/_4$ tsp
Meat tenderiser	2 tsp
Red colouring	$^1/_4$ tsp

METHOD

- Rinse ribs. Dry well with kitchen paper.

- Combine seasoning ingredients in a bowl. Add garlic, ginger and star anise. Mix well. Pour mixture over ribs and marinate for at least 8–10 hours (preferably overnight) in the refrigerator.

- Preheat oven at 220°C (440°F) for 15 minutes. Place ribs on a wire rack and roast for at least 1 hour, basting ribs with marinade occasionally and turning ribs over every 15 minutes.

- Heat the remaining marinade in a small saucepan over low heat and add maltose. Stir well until maltose dissolves.

- To coat ribs, dip them one by one into maltose mixture. Grill on each side for 3–5 minutes, or until well roasted.

VEGETABLES

Stir-fried Prawns with Cloud Ear Fungus and Snow Peas

Stir-fried Sweet and Sour Cabbage

Braised Dried Bean Curd with Dried Chinese Mushrooms

Bean Sprouts and Carrot with Salted Fish

Stir-fried Aubergines (Eggplants) with Minced Meat

STIR-FRIED PRAWNS WITH CLOUD EAR FUNGUS AND SNOW PEAS

Prawns stir-fried with cloud ear fungus and snow peas in chicken stock and light soy sauce.

Make a small slit on the back of the prawn. Use a pairing knife to remove black veins.

Stir-fry ingredients quickly to heat through.

Remove from heat once sauce bubbles to avoid overcooking prawns.

INGREDIENTS

Medium prawns (shrimps)	250 g (9 oz), peeled and deveined
Cooking oil	for deep-frying + 2 Tbsp
Snow peas	150 g (5 oz)
Garlic	2 cloves, peeled and finely chopped
Young ginger	2-cm (1-in) knob, peeled and finely chopped
Cloud ear fungus (*wan yee*)	10 large pieces, soaked to soften

SEASONING INGREDIENTS

Salt	1 tsp
Sugar	1/2 tsp
Egg white	1/2, beaten

SAUCE INGREDIENTS (COMBINED)

Chicken stock (page 32)	180 ml (6 fl oz / 3/4 cup)
Light soy sauce	1 Tbsp
Oyster sauce	1/2 Tbsp
Chinese rice wine	1/2 Tbsp
Corn flour (cornstarch)	2 tsp

METHOD

- Marinate prawns with seasoning ingredients for 30 minutes. Heat oil for deep-frying in a wok and blanch prawns in hot oil for 10 seconds. Drain and set aside.

- Reheat wok with 2 Tbsp cooking oil and stir-fry snow peas for 15 seconds. Drain and set aside.

- Add garlic and ginger to brown. Then add cloud ear fungus and prawns. Toss well.

- Combine ingredients for sauce and stir well. Pour over ingredients in wok and bring to the boil. Return snow peas and mix well before serving.

STIR-FRIED SWEET AND SOUR CABBAGE

A simple stir-fry of cabbage with chilli and peanut oil.

Cut Chinese celery cabbage into half lengthways then slice into 5-cm (2-in) strips.

Drain cabbage in a sieve. In the meantime, wipe the wok dry and carry on with the next step.

When sauce starts to bubble, add drained cabbage to the wok. Toss well so that cabbage will absorb sauce.

INGREDIENTS

Chinese celery cabbage (Chinese leaves)	700–900 g (1¹/₂ lb–1 lb 15¹/₂ oz)
Rice or wine vinegar	4–6 tsp
Sugar	4–6 tsp
Light soy sauce	4–6 tsp
Salt	a large pinch
Tapioca or potato flour	1–1¹/₂ tsp
Peanut or corn oil	4–5 Tbsp
Chillies	1 large or 2 small, seeded and cut into thread-like strips
Sesame oil	2–3 tsp for sprinkling

METHOD

- Remove any tough leaves from Chinese celery cabbage, halve the rest lengthways and slice across into 5-cm (2-in) strips.

- Combine vinegar, sugar, soy sauce, salt and tapioca or potato flour. Stir well and set aside.

- Heat a wok until hot, then add 2–3 Tbsp peanut or corn oil and swirl it around. Add cabbage and stir-fry continuously for 5–6 minutes. If the pieces begin to burn, lower heat. The cabbage bulk will decrease. Transfer to a colander and drain.

- Wipe the wok dry and reheat. Add remaining oil, swirl it around, then add chilli strips, stirring twice, and then add sauce. When sauce bubbles, add cabbage.

- Stir and toss well to let cabbage absorb sauce. When thoroughly hot, transfer to a warmed serving dish. Sprinkle sesame oil over cabbage and serve immediately.

BRAISED DRIED BEAN CURD WITH DRIED CHINESE MUSHROOMS

Dried mushrooms and broccoli add a distinctive flavour to this unique bean curd dish.

Use a paring knife to cut broccoli into small florets.

Add mushrooms to stir-fried ginger and shallots. Fry for a further 1–2 minutes.

Fry bean curd cubes in the wok, turning round until all sides are light brown in colour.

INGREDIENTS

Dried Chinese mushrooms	8–10, soaked until soft
Cooking oil	3 Tbsp
Ginger	2 slices, peeled and shredded
Shallot	1, peeled and sliced
Broccoli	90 g (3 oz), cut into small florets and rinsed
Dried bean curd cubes	250 g (9 oz)
Corn flour (cornstarch)	1 tsp, mixed with 1 Tbsp chicken stock or water
Sesame oil	1 tsp
Red chilli (optional)	1, sliced
Spring onion (scallion)	1, chopped

SEASONING INGREDIENTS

Salt	$1/4$ tsp
Sugar	$1/4$ tsp
Ground white pepper	$1/4$ tsp
Light soy sauce	1 tsp

SAUCE INGREDIENTS (COMBINED)

Chicken stock (page 32)	300 ml (10 fl oz / $1 1/4$ cups)
Dark soy sauce	$1/2$ Tbsp
Light soy sauce	2 tsp
Sugar	$1/2$ tsp
Salt	$1/4$ tsp
Ground white pepper	$1/4$ tsp

METHOD

- Season mushrooms with seasoning ingredients for 15 minutes.

- Heat $1 1/2$ Tbsp oil in a wok until and stir-fry ginger and shallots until fragrant, then add mushrooms and fry for another 1–2 minutes. Remove and set aside. Stir-fry broccoli for 1 minute, remove and set aside.

- Reheat remaining oil in the wok and toss bean curd cubes until crisp and light brown.

- Combine ingredients for sauce and stir well. Add to mushrooms and bring to the boil. Reduce heat and simmer for 10 minutes. Add broccoli and simmer for another 2 minutes.

- Thicken with corn flour mixture and sprinkle in sesame oil, red chillies and spring onion.

BEAN SPROUTS AND CARROT WITH SALTED FISH

Crispy bean sprouts stir-fried with shredded carrots and topped with salted fish.

INGREDIENTS

Salted fish	1 piece, about 5-cm (2-in) square
Cooking oil	4 Tbsp
Garlic	1 clove, peeled and chopped
Bean sprouts	450 g (1 lb)
Small carrot	1, peeled and shredded
Light soy sauce	1/2 Tbsp

METHOD

- Soak salted fish in water for a few minutes, then drain and slice thinly.

- Heat oil in a wok and brown garlic, then add salted fish. Fry until fragrant, then remove and set aside.

- Use the same oil to stir-fry bean sprouts and shredded carrot for about 2 minutes. Season with light soy sauce.

- Garnish with salted fish and serve immediately.

Peel small carrot. Cut into thin shreds.

Remove salted fish from water and drain. Use a cleaver to cut it into thin slices.

Add bean sprouts and carrot to the same wok and stir-fry for about 2 minutes.

STIR-FRIED AUBERGINES (EGGPLANTS) WITH MINCED MEAT

Aubergines fried with minced meat and hot bean paste served with spring onions and coriander leaves.

Drain aubergines and add to the wok. Turn up heat to stir-fry until soft.

Reheat wok and add garlic, ginger and hot bean paste. Continue to stir-fry until fragrant.

Pour chicken stock into wok. When stock starts to boil, return aubergines to wok and stir well to combine.

INGREDIENTS

Aubergines (eggplants/brinjals)	3, medium, cut into 5 x 1.25-cm (2 x ³/₄-in) pieces
Cooking oil	4 Tbsp
Garlic	6 cloves, peeled and minced
Ginger	3 slices, peeled
Hot bean paste	¹/₂ Tbsp
Lean pork with a little fat or chicken	120 g (4 oz), coarsely minced
Chicken stock (page 32)	125 ml (4 fl oz / ¹/₂ cup)
Corn flour (cornstarch)	¹/₂ Tbsp, mixed with 1 Tbsp water
Spring onions (scallions)	2, chopped
Coriander (cilantro) leaves	1 sprig, chopped

SAUCE INGREDIENTS (COMBINED)

Light soy sauce	1 Tbsp
Ground white pepper	¹/₄ tsp
Salt	¹/₄ tsp
Sugar	¹/₂ tsp
Sesame oil	1 tsp

METHOD

- Soak aubergines in a little salt water.

- Heat 3 Tbsp oil in a wok and brown 4 garlic cloves. Drain aubergines and add to the wok. Stir-fry over high heat until soft. Remove and set aside.

- Reheat wok with 1 Tbsp oil. Stir-fry remaining garlic, ginger and hot bean paste until fragrant. Add minced meat and when it changes colour, add combined sauce ingredients and stir-fry for 2 minutes.

- Pour in chicken stock and when it begins to boil, return pre-fried aubergines to the wok and stir to mix well.

- Thicken with corn flour mixture. Sprinkle in spring onions and coriander leaves before serving.

RICE &
NOODLES

Fried Yellow Noodles with Meat and Prawns

Fried Flat Rice Noodles with Beef

Rice Porridge

Fried Rice

Transparent Noodles and Fish Ball Soup

Steamed Chicken Glutinous Rice (*Lor Ma Kai*)

Pork Chow Mien

FRIED YELLOW NOODLES WITH MEAT AND PRAWNS

A complete meal of yellow noodles, meat and prawns in light gravy.

Place prawns in a mixing bowl and marinate well with salt, sugar, pepper and sesame oil.

After shallots are browned, add noodles to the wok and stir-fry for 1–2 minutes.

Pour combined sauce ingredients into the wok. Stir to mix well. Add in fried meat mixture and combine with noodles.

INGREDIENTS

Small prawns (shrimps)	120 g (4 oz), shelled, deveined and washed
Salt	¹/₄ tsp
Sugar	¹/₂ tsp
Dash of pepper and sesame oil	
Chicken or pork meat	120 g (4 oz), shredded
Light soy sauce	¹/₄ tsp
Corn flour (cornstarch)	¹/₂ tsp
Cooking oil	3 Tbsp
Garlic	2 cloves, peeled and minced
Mustard green (*choy sum*)	2 stalks, washed and cut into 5-cm (2-in) lengths
Shallots	4, peeled and sliced
Fresh yellow noodles	300 g (11 oz)
Corn flour (cornstarch)	1 tsp, mixed with 1 Tbsp water
Crisp-fried shallots	1 Tbsp
Spring onion (scallion)	1, chopped

SAUCE INGREDIENTS (COMBINED)

Chicken or pork bone stock	125 ml (4 fl oz / ¹/₂ cup)
Light soy sauce	1 Tbsp
Dark soy sauce	¹/₂ tsp
Sugar	¹/₂ tsp
Salt	¹/₄ tsp
Ground white pepper	¹/₄ tsp

METHOD

- Season prawns with salt, ¹/₄ tsp sugar, pepper and sesame oil. Season meat with light soy sauce, the remaining sugar and corn flour. Leave to marinate for at least 15 minutes.

- Heat 1 Tbsp oil in a wok and lightly brown garlic. Add meat, then prawns and toss until meat changes colour. Add mustard green and stir-fry for 1 minute. Remove and set aside.

- Reheat wok with 2 Tbsp oil and lightly brown shallots. Add noodles and stir-fry briskly for 1–2 minutes.

- Stir in combined sauce ingredients and return fried meat mixture to the wok. Stir well and thicken with corn flour mixture. Garnish with crisp-fried shallots and spring onion. Serve immediately.

FRIED FLAT RICE NOODLES WITH BEEF

Beef marinated in ginger juice and corn flour add colour and taste to fried flat rice noodles.

Using a pair of kitchen scissors, snip away both ends of mustard green.

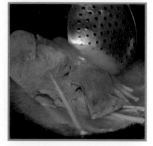

Scald mustard green very quickly then drain well.

When meat mixture is cooled, pour on top of noodles.

INGREDIENTS

Beef	120 g (4 oz), cut into thin slices
Cooking oil	6 Tbsp
Salt	$1/2$ tsp
Mustard green	5 small stalks, both ends trimmed
Fresh flat rice noodles	300 g (11 oz), loosened with fingers to separate strands
Light soy sauce	1 Tbsp, mixed with 1 Tbsp chicken stock or water
Bean sprouts	100 g ($3^1/2$ oz), tailed
Spring onion (scallion)	1, cut into 2.5-cm (1-in) lengths
Coriander leaves (cilantro)	1 sprig, cut into 2.5-cm (1-in) lengths

SEASONING INGREDIENTS

Bicarbonate of soda	$1/3$ tsp
Ginger juice	1 tsp
Salt	$1/2$ tsp
Sugar	$1/4$ tsp
Corn flour (cornstarch)	2 tsp

SAUCE INGREDIENTS (COMBINED)

Chicken stock (page 32)	5 Tbsp
Light soy sauce	$1/2$ tsp
Dark soy sauce	2 tsp
Corn flour (cornstarch)	3 tsp

METHOD

- Marinate beef with seasoning ingredients for at least 20 minutes.

- Bring half a saucepan of water to the boil. Add 1 Tbsp oil and salt. Scald mustard green until just cooked. Drain well and arrange on an oval dish. Turn off heat and scald beef. Allow to soak for 1 minute. Remove scum from surface, then drain meat and leave aside.

- Heat 1 Tbsp oil in a wok. Tip wok to ensure that it is well greased, then pour off excess oil. Add rice noodles and toss in hot wok for 2 minutes.

- Add light soy sauce mixture, and stir-fry until well mixed. Remove and place noodles on mustard green.

- Reheat wok with 1 Tbsp oil and stir-fry bean sprouts for 30 seconds. Remove and place over noodles.

- Wash wok and reheat with 1 Tbsp oil. Add combined sauce ingredients. Add meat, then spring onion and coriander leaves. Toss quickly, then add 2 Tbsp oil and mix well.

- Pour meat mixture over noodles. Serve with cut red chillies and light soy sauce.

RICE PORRIDGE

Soft-boiled rice served with pork, liver and fish slices.

Place rice in a pot and fill with adequate water to wash.

Add pork slices and stir into porridge.

Break a raw egg into the rice bowl then scoop boiling porridge over.

INGREDIENTS

Fish fillet (any kind)	450 g (1 lb), thinly sliced
Pork	90 g (3 oz), thinly sliced
Liver	60 g (2 oz), thinly sliced
Ginger juice	2 tsp
Rice wine	1 tsp
Light soy sauce	1 Tbsp
Long grain rice	225 g (8 oz)
Minced pork	120 g (4 oz)
Salt	to taste
Lard	1 Tbsp
Ground white pepper	to taste
Parsley	2 sprigs, chopped
Crisp-fried shallots	1 Tbsp

METHOD

- Season fish fillet, sliced pork and liver with ginger juice, rice wine, and soy sauce.

- Wash rice and boil in 1.5 litres (48 fl oz / 6 cups) water over medium heat for 30 minutes. Add minced pork, stir to mix well and boil over low heat for another 90 minutes, adding salt to taste.

- When rice is still boiling, add seasoned ingredients. Turn off heat immediately. Stir in lard. Serve in individual bowls, garnished with pepper, chopped parsley and crisp-fried shallots. If desired, a raw egg may be broken into each bowl before boiling porridge is ladled in.

FRIED RICE

Stir-fried rice with prawns, ham and peas garnished with egg strips.

Using a cleaver, chop spring onions into thin rounds. Sort out white and green rounds into separate parts.

Stir and toss prawns with a wooden spatula until they turn pinkish.

When frying rice, use a wooden spatula to turn and toss rice, starting from the bottom of the wok.

INGREDIENTS

Cooked rice	600 g (1 lb 5 oz)
Prawns (shrimps)	225 g (8 oz), shelled, deveined and cut into 2-cm (1-in) pieces
Cooking oil	8 Tbsp
Garlic	2 cloves, peeled and finely chopped
Shao Hsing wine or medium-dry sherry	1 Tbsp
Salt	
Freshly ground black pepper	to taste
Spring onions (scallions)	4, chopped, greens and whites separated
Eggs	2, beaten
Peas	225 g (8 oz)
Cooked ham	225 g (8 oz), diced
Dark soy sauce	1¹/₂ Tbsp
Chicken stock (page 32)	2–3 Tbsp
Dark soy sauce (optional)	1 tsp

MARINADE

Salt	¹/₂ tsp
Corn flour (cornstarch)	2¹/₂ tsp
Egg white	1 Tbsp

METHOD

- Combine marinade ingredients and stir in prawns. Coat evenly and refrigerate.

- Heat wok over high heat until it smokes. Add 2 Tbsp oil and swirl it around. Add garlic and when it browns, add prawns. When prawns turn pink, add wine or sherry along the rim of the wok. As soon as the sizzling dies down, remove prawns and set aside. Wash and dry the wok.

- Beat eggs lightly with 1 Tbsp oil and a little salt. Heat a large flat frying pan until moderately hot, add 1 Tbsp oil and swirl it around to cover the whole surface.

- Pour in half the beaten egg and tip the pan to spread egg evenly to the edges. When firm, turn egg over and fry the other side for a few seconds. Put egg on a plate and slice into strips.

- Stir cooked rice to loosen. Blanch peas in boiling water for 3 minutes and drain.

- Reheat wok over high heat until it smokes. Add remaining oil and swirl it around. Add white rounds of spring onion and stir.

- Pour in remaining egg and tip in rice. Toss well, separating any lumps.

- When rice is thoroughly hot, add ham and stir, then add peas and stir, and lastly add prawns. Still stirring, add soy sauce and stock. Stir in extra dark soy sauce for a more pronounced colour if desired. Finally, stir in half the egg strips. To serve, top with remaining egg strips and spring onions.

TRANSPARENT NOODLES AND FISH BALL SOUP

Transparent noodles add a different twist to this popular fish ball soup.

After soaking for 10 minutes, remove transparent noodles from water with a pair of chopsticks.

Heat up oil in a pot and stir-fry shallots and garlic to lightly brown them.

Add in fish balls to soup and boil for a further 2–3 minutes.

INGREDIENTS

Transparent noodles	45 g (1 1/2 oz), cut into 10-cm (4-in) lengths and soaked for 10 minutes and
Cooking oil	2 Tbsp
Shallots	2, peeled and sliced
Garlic	2 cloves, peeled and minced
Fresh anchovy or chicken stock (page 32)	1 litre (32 fl oz / 4 cups)
Preserved dried Chinese white cabbage (*tung choy*)	2 tsp, rinsed
Fish balls	15, medium, rinsed
Salt	to taste
Ground white pepper	to taste
Spring onions (scallions)	2, chopped

METHOD

- Drain softened transparent noodles and set aside.

- Heat oil in a pot and stir-fry shallots and garlic until lightly browned. Remove from oil and set aside.

- Pour in strained stock and bring to the boil. Add noodles and preserved dried Chinese white cabbage and boil for 5 minutes. Add fish balls and boil for another 2–3 minutes. Add salt and pepper to taste.

- Serve hot soup garnished with a sprinkling of shallot and garlic crisps and spring onions.

STEAMED CHICKEN GLUTINOUS RICE (LOR MA KAI)

Chicken richly-flavoured in oyster sauce, ginger juice and sesame oil is steamed covered in glutinous rice.

Ease meat away from bone with a pairing knife while holding bone with the other hand.

Press rice down after every spoonful to ensure that bowl is well-packed.

Be cautious when lifting the lid of the steamer to avoid scalding.

INGREDIENTS

Chicken	1, about 1.5 kg (3 lb 4$^1/_2$ oz)
Glutinous rice	1 kg (2 lb 3 oz)
Cooking oil	8 Tbsp
Dried Chinese mushrooms	60 g (2 oz), soaked and cut into strips
Shallots	8, peeled and sliced
Salt	2 tsp
Dark soy sauce	1 tsp
Five-spice powder	1 heaped tsp
Water	1 litre (32 fl oz / 4 cups)
Red chillies	2, seeded and sliced
Spring onions (scallions)	2, chopped
Coriander leaves (cilantro)	4 sprigs, cut into 2.5-cm (1-in) lengths
Chilli sauce	

SEASONING INGREDIENTS

Oyster sauce	4 Tbsp
Rice wine	2 tsp
Dark soy sauce	1 tsp
Light soy sauce	2 tsp
Ginger juice	2 tsp
Sesame oil	1 tsp
Sugar	1 tsp
Ground white pepper	$^1/_2$ tsp
Corn flour (cornstarch)	1 heaped tsp

METHOD

- Debone chicken and cut into 1.5-cm ($^3/_4$-in) thick slices. Season with seasoning ingredients for at least 1 hour.

- Wash and drain glutinous rice and steam for 45 minutes.

- Heat oil in a wok and fry mushrooms for 1–2 minutes. Drain from oil and leave aside.

- Lightly brown shallots and add glutinous rice, salt, dark soy sauce and five-spice powder and fry for 1 minute. Add water, mix well and simmer gently, covered, for 5–10 minutes. Remove from heat.

- Grease 12 medium rice bowls and add some fried mushrooms and seasoned chicken at the bottom of each bowl. Fill with glutinous rice and press with the back of a spoon to fill half of rice bowl.

- Steam over rapidly boiling water for 45 minutes.

- To serve, turn steamed glutinous rice onto a small dish. Garnish with chillies, spring onions and coriander leaves and serve hot with chilli sauce.

PORK CHOW MIEN

Chinese noodles fried with pork, mushrooms and prawns served with shredded lettuce.

Place noodles in a colander and run cold water through to prevent noodles from sticking.

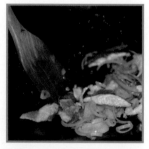

After stir-frying the onion, add pork and mushrooms and continue stir-frying.

Pour noodles into the wok and stir well to combine with the rest of the ingredients.

INGREDIENTS

Chinese noodles or spaghetti	225 g (8 oz)
Large prawns (shrimps)	100 g (3^1/$_2$ oz), boiled and shelled
Salt	to taste
Freshly ground black pepper	to taste
Vegetable oil	4 Tbsp
Onions	2 medium, peeled, halved and thinly sliced
Streaky pork	100 g (3^1/$_2$ oz), or leftover roast pork or lamb, cut into matchstick strips
Button mushrooms	3–4, cut into thick matchstick strips
Light soy sauce	3^1/$_2$ Tbsp
Dry sherry	3 Tbsp
Butter or lard	2 Tbsp
Large lettuce leaves	3, shredded

METHOD

- Boil noodles or spaghetti in salted water for 6–12 minutes or until just tender, then drain and rinse under cold water to separate strands. Season prawns with salt and pepper to taste.

- Heat oil in a wok over high heat. Add onions and stir-fry for 1 minute. Add pork and mushrooms and stir-fry with onions for 1 minute 30 seconds. Sprinkle over two-thirds of light soy sauce and stir-fry for another 1 minute 30 seconds. Reduce heat to medium.

- Add noodles or spaghetti to the wok and stir until all the ingredients are well mixed. Sprinkle in the remaining light soy sauce and half the sherry, reduce heat and simmer for 2–3 minutes.

- Heat butter or lard in a small frying-pan over medium heat. When it starts melting, add prawns and stir-fry for 1 minute 30 seconds. Add lettuce and stir-fry for 30 seconds. Place noodles in a large serving dish. Arrange prawns and lettuce on top and sprinkle with the remaining sherry to serve.

SWEETS

Gingko Nut and Water Chestnut Dessert

Sweet Dumplings

Sweet Yam Paste (*Au Nee*)

Peanut Crème

GINGKO NUT AND WATER CHESTNUT DESSERT

A sweet dessert made with gingko nuts and water chestnuts.

As rock sugar mixture is boiling, start to add in water chestnut cubes.

Pass flour mixture through strainer to refine.

Drizzle egg white into soup and stir with ladle at the same time.

INGREDIENTS

Water	1.5 litres (48 fl oz / 6 cups)
Rock sugar	300 g (11 oz)
Gingko nuts	180 g (6 oz), shelled and bitter centres removed
Water chestnuts	22, skinned and diced into 0.5-cm (^{1}/4-in) cubes
Egg whites	2, lightly beaten
Sweet potato flour	3 Tbsp
Corn flour (cornstarch)	1 Tbsp
Water	125 ml (4 fl oz / ^{1}/2 cup)

METHOD

- In a large saucepan, bring water and rock sugar to a slow boil. When rock sugar dissolves, add gingko nuts. Boil over low heat for 10 minutes, then add water chestnuts. Simmer for another 10 minutes.

- Combine sweet potato flour, corn flour and water, and strain mixture.

- Slowly drizzle and stir egg white into soup. Repeat with flour mixture. When it boils again, remove from heat.

- Serve hot or cold.

SWEET DUMPLINGS

Fried glutinous rice balls filled with delicious red bean paste.

Press a small piece of dough into a round shape then press a thumb into the centre.

Place 1 tsp bean paste in the centre then cover dough over bean paste.

Using a slotted spoon, scoop dumplings and drain them. Place dumplings onto a warmed serving plate.

INGREDIENTS

Cold water	225 ml (7$^1/_2$ fl oz)
Glutinous rice flour	225 g (8 oz)
Canned red bean paste	225 g (8 oz)
Water	1.5 litres (48 fl oz / 6 cups)
Cooking oil (optional)	as needed

METHOD

- Stir cold water gradually into the flour and work it into a smooth dough. There is no need to knead.

- Take a small piece of dough about the size of a chestnut and shape it into a ball. Press a thumb into the ball.

- Insert 1 tsp bean paste and work dough over bean paste completely: Roll dumpling between the palms to make it round. Repeat until all the dough and bean paste are used.

- Bring water to the boil in a large saucepan. Add about half the dumplings, one by one, and let water come back to the boil. Move dumplings once or twice with a wooden spoon to prevent them from sticking to the pan.

- Reduce the heat but continue to boil for 5–6 minutes or until dough looks transparent.

- Lift dumplings with a slotted spoon, drain and put them onto a warmed serving plate. Cook the rest of the dumplings in the same way, draining them thoroughly and putting them on the serving plate.

- Serve hot or, if wished, when they are drained, fry them in a little oil over medium low heat, gently stirring, until they begin to brown. This gives the sticky dumplings a delicious crisp outer coating.

- Dumplings can be frozen after step 3. It takes 8–9 minutes to cook them from frozen in boiling water and, again, they can be fried if wished.

SWEET YAM PASTE (AU NEE)

A tasty dessert of mashed yam, boiled gingko nuts and pumpkin.

INGREDIENTS

Gingko nuts	115 g (4 oz), shelled and washed
Sugar	227 g (8 oz)
Pumpkin	225 g (8 oz), diced into 2-cm (1-in) cubes
Yam	900 g (2 lb), diced into 5-cm x 1-cm (2 x ¹/₂-in) cubes
Castor sugar	12 Tbsp
Lard	6 Tbsp
Shallots	3, peeled and sliced thinly

METHOD

- Boil 2 Tbsp water and add gingko nuts and half the sugar over low heat for 45 minutes until sugar is absorbed into nuts. Add water a little at a time while cooking. Cool and cut gingko nuts in half, removing centre fibre if any.

- Boil another 2 Tbsp water and add remaining sugar and pumpkin cubes Cook until sugar is absorbed. Add a little water at a time while cooking to prevent sugar from burning. Set gingko nuts and pumpkins aside.

- Steam yam pieces over rapidly boiling water until very soft. Combine half of the yam, 2 Tbsp lard and half of the castor sugar in a food processor until smooth. Remove to a bowl and repeat with remaining yam, another 2 Tbsp lard and remaining castor sugar.

- Heat the remaining lard in a wok to fry sliced shallots until very lightly browned. Add yam paste and stir-fry over low heat for 30 seconds. Remove to a shallow serving bowl. Place cooked pumpkin cubes around sides of the bowl and arrange gingko nuts over yam paste. Serve hot.

Using a pairing knife, cut gingko nuts into halves and remove the fibre within.

Mash half of the yam with oil and sugar. Continue mashing until texture is smooth.

After shallots are lightly browned, add in yam paste and stir-fry over low heat.

PEANUT CRÈME

Blended peanuts and rice boiled with sugar and water is a perfect dessert to round off a meal.

INGREDIENTS

Peanuts	625 g (1 lb 6 oz), shelled
Rice	2 Tbsp, washed and drained
Water	2 litres (64 fl oz / 8 cups)
Sugar	310 g (11 oz)

METHOD

- Roast peanuts until light brown. Remove skin.

- Using an electric blender, blend rice and half of the peanuts with 455 ml (14 fl oz / 1¾ cups) water until very fine. Add 2–3 Tbsp water if necessary to keep mixture moving and rotating. Pour into a bowl and set aside.

- Repeat process using the other half of the peanuts with another 455 ml water (14 fl oz / 1¾ cups).

- Place blended peanuts, sugar and remaining water in a heavy-bottomed aluminium saucepan. Bring to the boil over a moderate heat, stirring mixture continuously with a wooden spoon. Simmer for 5 minutes, stirring continuously. Remove from heat. Serve hot or cold.

Place peanuts in a wok and roast until light brown.

Blend rice and half portion of the peanuts with water in an electric blender. Process until very fine.

Bring mixture to the boil over moderate heat, making sure to stir continuously with a wooden spoon.

GLOSSARY
& INDEX

GLOSSARY

BAMBOO SHOOTS

Canned bamboo shoots are convenient to use but remember to rinse them thoroughly before use. If using fresh bamboo shoots, peel off outer skin and cut away the tough fibrous layer. Then boil the shoots in slightly salted water with $1/2$ Tbsp of sugar for about 30 minutes. Boil in fresh water for 15 minutes. Bamboo shoots can keep up to 2 weeks if properly frozen.

BROCCOLI

When choosing broccoli, pick the dark green ones with a firm and closely-packed head. The harder parts of the stems can be pared and then sliced for cooking. Before stir-frying broccoli, blanch it in boiling salted water with a little oil first to cook it slightly. Alternatively, you can toss it in a little hot oil for a minute or two.

BEAN CURD

Bean curd, made from soy beans, comes in many forms. Soft bean curd is sold as white squares or rectangles of curd immersed in water. There is also a circular type that is sold in plastic tubes, known as Japanese taufu. They should be able to keep for a few days. Bean curd cubes that have been fried in oil are called taufu pok.
Bean curd can be made into yellowish translucent sheets called bean curd sheets (*foo pei*). It is commonly used for wrapping meat and vegetable fillings. Make sure you buy the soft and flexible sheets because the brittle ones are inappropriate for wrapping.

Dried soy bean sticks (*foo chok*) are yellow in colour. They are often used in mixed vegetable dishes. They have to be soaked in warm water prior to use.

Soft salted bean curd cubes (*lam yee*) are kept preserved in a brine and wine solution with chillies. They have a distinctive flavour and complements porridge very well.

CELERY

Look for crisp light green celery with young stalks when choosing. Avoid using very large stalks since they may be fibrous. The fibres will require removing before slicing the stalk into smaller pieces.

CHINESE DATES

Red dates are dark red in colour and have a sweet taste. They should be slit then added to soups and stews, so that their full flavour can be released. The Chinese believe that red dates are good for anaemics.

CORIANDER LEAVES (CILANTRO)

Coriander is also known as Chinese parsley. The leaves have a strong flavour and are usually used for flavouring and garnishing food. The flavour is different from English parsley so you should not use it as a substitute but it is acceptable as garnishing.

DRIED PRAWNS (SHRIMPS)

These small prawns are very flavourful, so they are usually added to vegetable and soup dishes to enhance their taste. They are dried so you need to soak them in water to soften and rinse before using.

FERMENTED BLACK BEANS

Fermented black beans or black bean sauce is sold in small plastic packets. Made from salted and fermented black soy beans, they have a very strong flavour so it is best to use sparingly. Before using, soak them in water for 5–10 minutes then rinse and drain thoroughly. Fermented black beans are used in both meat and seafood dishes.

GALANGAL

Native to Southern China, galangal is from the same family as ginger but it cannot be used to substitute ginger. It is commonly used for making medicinal herbal mixtures and to cover up the strong flavour of meats like duck and lamb.

GARLIC

Garlic is used in Chinese cooking to flavour oil, especially when stir-frying. Make sure that you only use fresh garlic. Garlic powder and flakes are inadequate substitutes for fresh garlic.

GINGER

The pungent ginger root is used to reduce the strong flavours in meat and the 'fishy' smells in fish. Two types of ginger are used in Chinese cooking, young ginger and old ginger. Young ginger, as compared to old ginger, is juicer, less pungent and has a paler skin colour. Before using ginger, you have to peel off the skin by scraping it with a paring knife. Then cut it according to the recipe. If fresh ginger is unavailable, it is better to omit it than to use dried or powdered ginger as a substitute.

GINGKO NUTS

This yellow almond-shaped nut is commonly used as either a savoury stuffing or in sweet soups. It is quite firm but becomes soft and tender once it is cooked. You can buy it shelled or unshelled. Before using, cut it open with a paring knife to remove the bitter centre vein. Gingko nut is believed to be good for asthma, coughs, weak bladders and urinary disorders.

HOT BEAN PASTE

This spicy sauce is a made from a mix of fermented soy beans and chillies. It is also known as chilli bean sauce or hot soy bean sauce.

MUSHROOMS (TUNG KU)

There are several different types of mushrooms used in Chinese cooking. They are champignon or button mushrooms (*mou ku*), straw mushrooms and dried Chinese mushrooms.

You can easily find fresh champignon or canned button mushrooms in supermarkets. Choose the white unblemished ones and when preparing, do not peel off the skin unless it is bruised. They usually cook in about 5 minutes and are good for combining with meats and other vegetables. They are also delicious when used in soups.

Straw mushrooms (*tsin cho ku*) have been named as such because they are cultivated in straw. You can buy them either fresh or canned, but fresh ones have to be scalded before use. After scalding, they can be only stored in the refrigerator for a few days.

There are two varieties of dried Chinese mushrooms, the winter mushroom (*tung ku*) and the flower mushroom (*fah ku*). The former is thick and greyish black in colour while the latter is paler in colour and more expensive. Before cooking, soak them in water for at least 30 minutes to soften. Reserve the stems for flavouring stocks, especially for strict vegetarian cooking. Remove the stems, wash, dry and grind with a pepper mill or an electric blender until fine for the stock. To store for a long period of time, ensure that they are well dried before blending and store in the refrigerator in an air-tight container.

MUSTARD GREEN (CHOY SUM)

Choy Sum is a green leafy vegetable with light green stems. It is suitable for frying with noodles because it is crunchy and juicy but it is equally tasty when fried on its own or made into a soup.

Mustard green is also used pickled to make salty pickled mustard green (*harm mui choy*) and slightly sweet pickled mustard green (*tim mui choy*). Both of these are partially dried. Before use, you need to wash carefully and constantly change the water to get rid of fine sand particles.

Dried mustard green (*choy korn*) is used to make soups. It has to be soaked until softened and washed carefully prior to use.

NOODLES

To the Chinese, the length of noodles symbolises longevity. Chinese noodles are available in a variety of forms, from thin strands to thick broad ribbons that are either fresh or dried. They vary in terms of taste and texture so you should only use the particular noodle called for in the recipe. The commonly used ones are yellow noodles and egg noodles. Yellow noodles are made from flour, alkaline water and yellow colouring while egg noodles contain an additional ingredient of eggs. Transparent noodles (*tang hoon*), also known as bean thread noodles, is a type of thin strand noodles made from mung beans. It is often used in vegetarian dishes and in soups. Before using, you should soak it in water to soften first.

RICE VERMICELLI

Rice is made into long thin strands of white dried noodles to make rice vermicelli. Before using, it has to be softened first, by soaking in water if stir-frying or by scalding briefly if adding to a soup.

ROCK SUGAR

Rock sugar is actually crystallised sugar sold in rock-like lumps. It is less sweet than granulated sugar.

SESAME SEEDS

In Chinese cooking, white sesame seeds are used either roasted or raw to make sweets and fillings, or as garnishing in savoury dishes. It is also sold as a creamy paste available at supermarkets.

RICE

Rice is the staple food of the Chinese people. Long grain rice is of better quality so always use it when available. In addition, old rice is preferred to new rice because it will not stick together when cooked.

SALTED CABBAGE (HARM CHOY)

Salted cabbage is made by salting and pickling green stem vegetables. You should wash it thoroughly and soak it in water to reduce the salt content before use. It is most commonly used in duck soup but it can also be fried with meat.

SNOW PEAS

Snow peas are flat pea pods that are light green in colour. Before cooking, you have to wash and soak them in water to prevent the peas from splitting when cooked. After cooking, break the ends of the pod slightly to remove the fibre from the side edges of the pea pods.

SICHUAN VEGETABLE (CHAR CHOY)

These Sichuan vegetable is actually preserved Chinese radish pickled in salt and chillies. When you buy it, you can still see the chilli powder coating the olive green coloured vegetable. Before using it, you have to wash it carefully and leave it to soak in water to reduce its saltiness.

SOUR PLUMS

These marble-sized, light brown plums have been pickled in vinegar and salt. They are usually used when steaming fish to add a sour tang.

SOY BEAN PASTE (TAU CHEO)

Soy bean paste is available in two forms, as whole soy beans or in purée form. The paste is light brown in colour.

STAR ANISE

This is a brown coloured, star-shaped spice that is actually the fruit of the oriental evergreen of the magnolia family which is native to China and Japan. It has a strong and distinctive smell so all you need is a small amout to flavour meat, poultry and duck dishes.

WATER CHESTNUT

The water chestnut has a sweet taste and is firm and crunchy. It is available in both fresh and canned form. It is also available in powder form, which is used to thicken soups.

WHITE CABBAGE (PAK CHOY)

The Chinese white cabbage is a long leaf cabbage with green leaves. It has a bland taste and is quite watery. There is also a shorter variety with light green stems called Shanghai white cabbage (*siew pak choy*).

INDEX

A

aubergines 84

B

bamboo shoots 18, 32
    canned 18
bean curd 32, 80
    firm bean curd 80
    soft bean curd 32
Bean Curd Hot Pot 32
Bean Sprouts and Carrot with
    Salted Fish 82
Beef Patties in Tomato Sauce 58
bell pepper 22
Braised Dried Bean Curd with
    Dried Chinese Mushrooms 80
Braised Fish Head with Black
    Bean Sauce 52
Butter Prawns with Toasted
    Coconut 46

C

Chicken Stew with Fresh
    Chestnuts 60
Chilli Oyster Crabs 42
Chinese rice wine 16, 18, 20
Chinese sausage 20
Claypot Fish Head 54
cloud ear fungus 76
Crab Omelette 48

D

Deep-fried Pork Rolls 18
Deep-fried Five Spice Rolls 24
dried prawns 22
Duck and Salted Vegetable Soup
    28

F

Fried Garlic Pork 62
Fried Oyster Fritters 50
Fried Rice 94
Five-Spice Crispy Skin Chicken
    64
five-spice powder 24, 64
Fried Flat Rice Noodles with Beef
    90
Fried Meat and Vegetable
    Dumplings 16
Fried Yellow Noodles with Meat
    and Prawns 88

G

Ginger Chicken in Earthen Pot 68
gingko nut 104, 108
Gingko Nut and Water Chestnut
    Dessert 104
glutinous rice 98
glutinous rice flour 106

H

Hot Sour Soup 34

N

noodles
    fresh flat rice noodles 90
    fresh yellow noodles 88
    transparent noodles 96

O

Old Cucumber and Pork Soup 30

P

pickled sour plum 28
Peanut Crème 110

Pig's Trotters in Chinese Black
    Vinegar 66
Pork Chow Mien 100
Prawn Wantan Soup 36

R

rice vermicelli 48
Rice Porridge 92
Roast Pork Ribs 72

S

Sea Bass with Spicy Black
    Vinegar Sauce 44
Steamed Chicken Glutinous Rice
    (Lor Ma Kai) 98
Steamed Mushrooms with Prawn
    Filling 20
Stir-fried Aubergines (Eggplants)
    with Minced Meat 84
Stir-fried Sichuan Style Squid 40
Stir-fried Prawns with Cloud Ear
    Fungus and Snow Peas 76
Stir-fried Sweet and Sour
    Cabbage 78
Stuffed Capsicums (Bell Peppers)
    22
Sweet Dumplings 106
Sweet Yam Paste (Au Nee) 108

T

Teochew Duck 70
Transparent noodles and Fish
    Ball Soup 96

W

water chestnut 20, 24
white cabbage 16